Norfolk Railways

NORFOLK RAILWAYS c. 1920 (NOT TO SCALE)

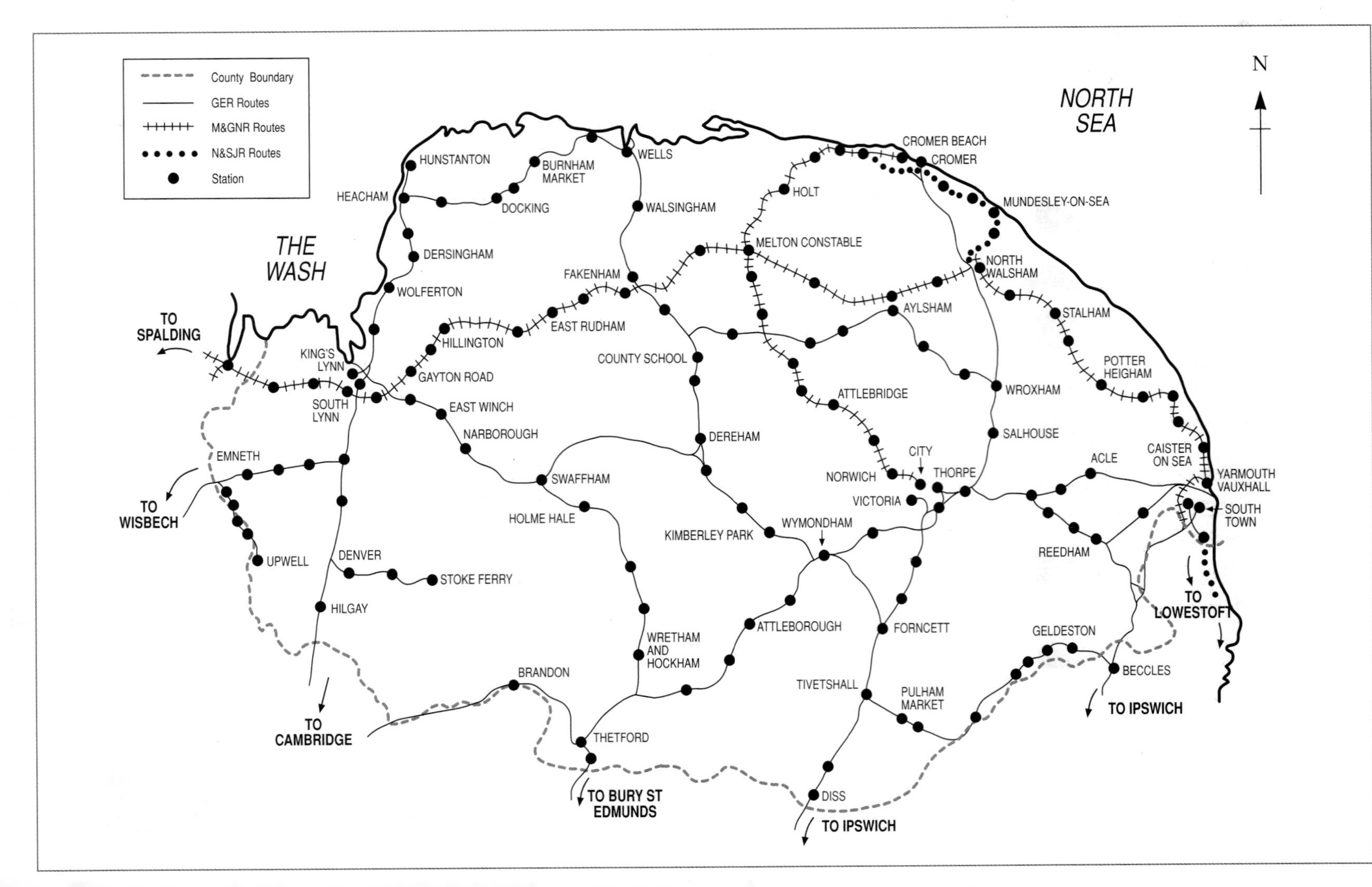

Norfolk Railways

WILLIAM H. SMITH

SUTTON PUBLISHING LIMITED

Sutton Publishing Limited
Phoenix Mill · Thrupp · Stroud
Gloucestershire · GL5 2BU

First published 2000

Title Page: GER T26/2–4–0 No 441 'Little Sharpie' at Cromer Station, *c.* 1905. (HMRS/R. Hilton Collection)

British Library Cataloguing in Publication Data
A catalogue record for this book is available from the British Library.

ISBN 0-7509-2308-3

Typeset in 10.5/13.5 Photina.
Typesetting and origination by
Sutton Publishing Limited.
Printed and bound in England by
J.H. Haynes & Co. Ltd, Sparkford.

Contents

The M&GNR Preservation Society special at Aylsham (distinguished as 'South' since September 1948). This train was the first passenger train to run over the curve at Themelthorpe which connected the Wroxham County School line to the ex-M&GN Norwich City branch thereby cutting 24 miles off the distance between Norwich City and Norwich Thorpe by rail. (They were only about one mile apart by road.) *(B.P. Hoper Collection)*

Introduction

Although the Norfolk, Suffolk and Essex Railroad scheme to connect Norfolk with London was abandoned, it did at least mean that the county was not entirely left out of the first great railway promotion boom of the mid-1820s.

By the 1830s the second great upsurge in railway investment had begun, and the Eastern Counties Railway (ECR) was incorporated (1836) to build a trunk line from London to Norwich and Great Yarmouth. Much of the money involved in this came from outside Norfolk, Liverpool's pioneering railway investors' interests, in particular, subscribing heavily.

The land that was needed by the ECR for their route between Great Yarmouth and Norwich could not be bought, so in 1839 the ECR was forced to construct at the London end only.

Losing faith in the ECR to deliver a railway to Yarmouth, local industrialists, bankers and solicitors such as Sir Edmund Lacon started the Yarmouth and Norwich Railway (Y&NR), whose plan was given the Royal assent in June 1842.

In due course, nationally known railway builders George Stephenson (chairman) and his son Robert (engineer) became involved in Norfolk with the Y&NR line. Another giant of the mid-Victorian railway scene, Sir Samuel Morton Peto, also turned his attention to Norfolk (as contractor for the Y&NR, with his cousin Thomas Grissell), eventually becoming MP for Norwich. George Bidder, famous in his youth as 'the calculating boy' for his precocious mathematical abilities, was yet another from the railway Hall of Fame to become associated with Norfolk railways through his participation as engineer to the Y&NR. Typically, these contracts employed many labourers or navvies to dig and build the earthworks, 1,500 in the case of the Y&NR. In Norfolk, as in other counties, the general fear of the railway navvies escalated into a 'bogeyman' image, usually undeservedly; no doubt the influx of such numbers of strangers into the tranquil Norfolk countryside must have caused notable excitement, if nothing else.

On 1 May 1844 the Y&NR, which had cost £10,000 per mile to build, opened for regular passenger services, and the so-called 'mania' to construct railways had begun for a third successive decade. It was an apparently easy way for those who could afford to invest to increase their wealth at a time of national economic recovery.

The Y&NR had still not made the railway connection with the capital that was seen by 1845 as economic necessity; so, instead of looking south eastwards to Colchester, Norfolk's railway promoters turned to seek out the Northern and Eastern line from London to Cambridge. They planned to meet up with an extension of this line at Brandon. This achieved, under the title of the Norfolk and Brandon Railway– and once the swing bridge over the River Wensum at Trowse was operational in December 1845 – Norwich and Yarmouth finally succeeded in their ambition to have a London connection, 123 miles long, albeit not the direct route that some would have preferred.

'Lynn is making great efforts to connect itself with the extensive Railways now traversing the kingdom', stated literature published prior to the authorisation in 1845 of both the Lynn and Ely and Lynn and Dereham Railways (later amalgamated as the East Anglian Railway). Between them these companies would carry out the intentions of citizens of King's Lynn who, until the line to Ely was built, had to rely upon a horse-drawn day coach along poorly maintained roads if they wanted to reach London.

Having achieved the desired railway connection with London, attention in Norfolk then turned to other parts of the 'kingdom'; and, with the opening of the Eastern Counties line from Ely to Peterborough, by 1847 Norfolk was also joined by rail to the Midlands and the North. Just before the Norwich and Brandon Railway was opened, that company and the Yarmouth and Norwich Railway had amalgamated in 1845 to become the Norfolk Railway (NR). The NR built branches to Lowestoft and Fakenham, became an early user of the telegraph to pass on information, but nevertheless earned a poor image through an unfortunate safety record. Leasing by the ECR in 1848 was intended to put matters right, but did not; and it took until 1856–7, with a major reconstruction of the route, for remedies to work.

The direct route to London from Norwich had been thwarted by the ECR's decision to terminate at Colchester which caused concern not only in Norwich but

Left: Ex-M&GN somersault distant signal with a concrete post at Massingham, 22 February 1959. Some signals in the 1870s were operated with a signal arm fixed inside a slotted post. One such became frozen into its slot and the false indication caused a serious accident in 1876. Edward French of the GNR was motivated by this event to solve the problem with a centre balanced, or somersault, arm. *(Philip Kelley)*

in Ipswich too. There, entrepreneurs including the Cobbold family activated a scheme called the Eastern Union Railway (EWR), which employed another great Victorian engineer, Joseph Locke, who assisted on the extension to Norwich opened in December 1849. This apparent advantage to Norwich and Norfolk turned sour upon the obstructionist attitude of the ECR's management, who went as far as to state that their intention was to destroy EUR traffic by their tactics at Colchester.

In spite of good traffic receipts, high running expenses drove EUR into an agreement with the opposition that from 1 January 1854, the ECR would work both the EUR and the Norfolk Railway.

By the middle of the nineteenth century, the Norfolk landscape included the smoke of the passing steam trains as they contributed to a new mobility for people and products. The railway made its mark on village life, with many now acquiring a local railway station, possibly with its connecting omnibus, and thriving hotels taking their names from the new phenomenon, such as the Railway Arms at Reedham, the Railway Hotel at Wymondham and numerous Railway Taverns around the county. Coal, the underlying driving force of Victorian industrial

Kimberley Park station looking towards Dereham, *c.* 1939. The Dereham branch opened for freight on 3 December 1846 and for passengers on 15 February 1847, though it is not certain that Kimberley, as it was known, opened at this time. The name change came on 1 July 1923. In the picture the original Norfolk railway building is to the left, furthest from camera, with GER additions of 1882 nearer the camera. The GER monogram can be made out in the ironwork and bench supports. (*Stations UK)*

prosperity, became available cheaply and in bulk. Two decades of affluence within the farming industry were supported by the coming of the railways to transport produce to ever-expanding markets within and outside Norfolk.

Of course, there were some losers; the cattle drovers became redundant, for instance, with consequent effects on suppliers of lairage and accommodation. The stage coach lost out to the new, speedier competition: river and coastal transport was too slow and unreliable in comparison, whilst those responsible for the poorly maintained public highways were forced to consider their improvement for the future. Railway investment was not all sweetness and light however. A collapse in the money market in the late 1840s led to large losses of money paid by some unfortunate individuals into abandoned schemes.

FORMATION OF THE GER

A watershed in the history of Norfolk's railways occurred in 1862 when a company was formed that was to manage a large proportion of the county's railway network for the next sixty years. This was the Great Eastern Railway (GER), amalagamated from the ECR, the EUR, the Norfolk, the East Anglian and East Suffolk Railways. At its inception it had a short-lived monopoly of railway transport in Norfolk; and, although taking over the financial shortcomings of the units it was formed from nearly caused its own demise, by the 1880s it had turned an economic corner and served Norfolk well in railway terms.

The GER did what it could to encourage the agricultural trade when a downturn for arable farmers developed in the last decades of the nineteenth century. It greatly assisted in the establishment of a Norfolk tourist industry at the same time. The fashionable 'Poppyland' holiday phenomenon of the North Norfolk coast, for instance, was materially supported by the Great Eastern's board with the railway's associated property company having a large input into the development of Hunstanton. The West Norfolk Railway was an good example of GER operations in Norfolk. Initially providing support, particularly financial, for the scheme, the GER operated the line for a share of the receipts before buying the company from the Hunstanton and West Norfolk Railway in 1890.

In contrast, a line independent of the GER had opened between 1879 and 1881 from Yarmouth to North Walsham, followed by the Lynn and Fakenham which then merged with the Yarmouth and North Norfolk and the Yarmouth Union to form the Eastern and Midlands Company, creating a joined-up route across North Norfolk in competition with the GER – even to the extent of including a branch into Norwich and one to Cromer. The similarly named Midland and Eastern Railway was then absorbed by the EMR extending their control westwards from King's Lynn towards Spalding and Sutton Bridge and finally, in 1883, the Peterborough, Wisbech and Sutton Bridge route completed the valuable link to the English coalfields for the EMR.

The MR and GNR already had interests west of King's Lynn in the sense that they worked lines in this district, so that, when the EMR went into receivership in 1890, the MR and GNR agreed to purchase it and form, at 183 miles, the longest joint-owned railway in the UK, to become known from 1893 as the Midland and Great Northern Railway. With its headquarters at Melton Constable, the village soon developed into a railway town through the influence of the M&GN and its ground breaking engineer and locomotive superintendent, William Marriot, along with the support of the local landowner, Lord Hastings.

The competition that the M&GNR provided for the GER did little to alter the ethos of paternalistic support for the varied aspirations of the communities that they served that was prevalent amongst the enlightened GER directors, such as Lord Claud Hamilton. In one instance, competition turned to co-operation between the two rival companies when the Norfolk and Suffolk Joint Committee was formed in 1898 for the development of Norfolk's north east coast.

PIONEERING ATTEMPT

By the turn of the century the GER had a stable financial background and was able to pay a high level of dividend to its shareholders while establishing, as the new century dawned, a pioneering attempt at transport integration with a bus service linked to the railway's passenger service, as well as continuing its diversification into shipping undertakings.

The onset of the First World War stimulated the use and development of the internal combustion engine so that, after the Armistice, lorries and buses became available and were soon commonplace as competitors on the roads of Norfolk in the 1920s along with a growing number of privately owned cars.

At the Grouping, in 1923, Parliamentary authority released the railways from wartime government control, and as a result the newly created London and North Eastern Railway took over the GER's role in Norfolk whilst the M&GNR became jointly managed by the LMS and LNER at first; until, in 1936, the LNER took over all local administration.

The 1920s and '30s were difficult times for the LNER in Norfolk. In spite of attempts to stimulate holiday traffic to the coast and to the Broads, annual passenger figures showed a decline, as did agricultural traffic. The Second World War created the need for and establishment of military installations within the county, while the important contribution to the war effort made by the farming industry created a real though short-lived, upsurge in the activities of Norfolk railwaymen (and by this time, in greater numbers, railwaywomen).

No doubt the crowing of locomotive whistles could be heard at midnight on 31 December 1947 around Norfolk as elsewhere in response to the optimism felt by the rank and file railwaymen at the concept of nationalisation scheduled to start the next day. The four railway groups became part of British Railways, Norfolk being placed in the Eastern Region. Very little changed immediately. The liveries altered, but much quite elderly pre-grouping rolling stock, some carriages still lit by gas, was in use around Norfolk, particularly in branch line service, and the ex-LMS influence on the old M&GN lines was still apparent.

A turning point in Norfolk's railways came in 1955, when BR introduced wholesale diesel traction for passenger haulage – particularly the diesel multiple units aimed at economising on the costs of branch and short cross-country passenger services, thereby retaining their viability. However, the M&GN lines were not saved by the new developments and became early closure victims in 1959, at the very start of what has become known as the Beeching era when the publication of a report entitled *The Reshaping of British Railways* paved the way for a run-down of services, followed by closure of miles of Norfolk's railways as part of a nationwide policy.

Following a depressing time for railway transport in general, in the 1970s a new spirit of enterprise produced an upsurge in belief in the future of what remained of Norfolk's rail network. The steam engine had by now been totally replaced by diesel and overhead electric power. Today, along with privatisation and the start of a new century, yet more re-invigoration of Norfolk's railway heritage seems possible with schemes such as a proposed Norfolk Orbital Railway reaching the public domain as a feasibility study during the autumn of 2000.

1

North East Norfolk

GER Class T26 2–4–0 No 441 departing from Cromer on an Up train of 6-wheeled carriages to Norwich, *c.* 1905. This terminal was opened by the East Norfolk Railway on 26 March 1877 and was situated high above the town as can be detected in this view. *(HMRS/R. Hilton)*

WHITLINGHAM TO CROMER

The East Norfolk Railway was incorporated in 1864 to serve the area between the Norwich to Yarmouth and Wymondham to Wells lines working in alliance with the GER. The GER could not afford to build the infrastructure of the line but were agreeable to running the trains on behalf of the ENR for 50 per cent of the receipts. Construction work started from a junction at Whitlingham in 1865 but, as work began, the time coincided with the disastrous failure of the bankers Overend and Gurney which affected the confidence of investors into railways in particular. During the economic crisis that followed in 1866, construction work on the North Walsham line, like other projects caught up in the maelstrom, fell into abeyance.

In the same era, the Norfolk coast was in the earliest throes of its establishment as a fashionable holiday destination for the Victorian middle classes. Opening a railway line reaching the coast assumed a greater financial incentive to prospective shareholders and the northwards extension to Cromer was included in the powers, granted by Parliament in 1872, to allow further time for completion to North Walsham.

A 14 mile-long single track was opened to North Walsham in October 1874 and extended to Gunton on 29 July 1876 followed by further construction to Cromer by 26 March 1877.

Between Whitlingham Junction and North Walsham, small wooden stations were established at Salthouse, Wroxham and Worstead and with no severe engineering problems to overcome, this single line section was opened for passenger traffic operated by the GER on 21 October 1874. Goods services followed in March 1875 and a small profit was declared after the first half year's trading.

The GER absorbed the line under an Act of 1881 and the line was doubled between Whitlingham and North Walsham by 1900. Competition from the arrival at Cromer in 1887 of the rival Eastern and Midlands Railway caused an improved timetable leading to the instigation in 1897 of the Cromer Express, non-stop in each direction to North Walsham daily in the summer from Liverpool Street station, reaching Cromer in 2 hours 55 minutes. This train was developed to include three restaurant cars from 1899 and with a change of name to the Norfolk Coast Express it became the GER's blue riband train, including portions for Mundesley and for Sheringham. It was the Edwardian era, when the coast enjoyed the Poppyland image created by writer Clement Scott.

Passenger traffic and that generated by agriculture remained buoyant throughout the LNER period when the luxury Eastern Belle Pullman was in its pomp.

Under British Railways' management, summer holiday traffic was at first maintained with titled trains such as the Broadsman, reflecting the popularity of the Norfolk Broads and creating good passenger ticket sales at Wroxham station, for instance. However other traffic suffered a decline and the former GER station at Cromer, distinguished as High Cromer from September 1948, closed to passenger traffic in 1954 and trains ran into the ex-M&GN station at Cromer Beach. As elsewhere, the trend towards holiday destinations outside the UK brought an end to the seasonal holiday traffic by 1968, leaving only a remnant of local passenger trains.

DEREHAM TO WELLS

This line was the north eastern section and most distinct part of a route through to Wells-next-the-Sea from Wymondham. In turn, the Dereham to Wells line could be appraised as two parts: Dereham to Fakenham, opened as part of the Norfolk Railway on 20 March 1849, and the Wells and Fakenham Railway, opened on 1 December 1857, under the patronage of the Earl of Leicester, being the product of a local company using the names of the two towns. A branch to Wells Harbour was enabled under an Act of 1859. This harbour did not develop to the significance once anticipated and Wells could not rival towns such as Cromer as a holiday resort. Dereham to Wells remained very much a farmers' line until a mini-boom in trippers took place in the 1950s; but it was insufficiently imposing to rescue the economic situation. Subsequently, the harbour branch became redundant and there followed closure to passengers on 3 October 1964, then to goods on 31 October 1964.

WROXHAM TO COUNTY SCHOOL BRANCH

The East Norfolk Railway was also responsible for the development of the branch from Wroxham to Aylsham and County School. This route of just above 23 miles opened in stages; from Wroxham to Buxton Lamas on 8 July 1879, to Aylsham on 1 January 1880, to Cawston on 1 September 1880, to Reepham on 2 May 1881 and finally to

County School and a junction with the Dereham–Wells line on 1 May 1882. The leisurely pace of construction in some way demonstrated the nature of the undertaking, which was largely territorial to prevent incursions by rivals into this area of Norfolk.

When BR took over, passenger trains on the route were withdrawn early on 15 September 1952. Goods services were withdrawn on the same day between Reepham and Foulsham. The Foulsham to County School goods service held out longer, until 31 October 1964. Themelthorpe curve opened on 12 September 1960 and provided a link between the ex-ENR branch near Reepham and the ex-MGN line at Whitwell which served Norwich City station until its closure in 1969, leaving freight traffic only to Lenwade.

MELTON CONSTABLE TO CROMER BEACH

The M&GNR branch between Melton Constable to Cromer via Sheringham opened on 1 October 1884 to Holt, four years after the Act that empowered it, and was followed by an extension to Cromer, opened 16 June 1887 under a second Act of 1882. The terminal station at Cromer Beach was far more conveniently situated than the GER station and by collaborating with the Great Northern Railway a daily through service between King's Cross and Cromer via Peterborough and Sutton Bridge was established. The GER maintained running rights to Sheringham from July 1906 and daily until 1962. Through coaches to Liverpool Street station were also in the timetable, shrinking to summer Saturdays-only prior to closure. Passenger services between Melton Constable and Sheringham survived until 6 April 1964, freight until the end of that year when the line closed completely under British Rail. The preservationist movement then began to restore a section of line under the title of the North Norfolk Railway.

The Norfolk and Suffolk Joint Railways

The N&SR was a joint initiative set up in 1898 by the M&GNR and the GER aimed at serving the developing holiday coastline of the Cromer district, first opened up to railway connection by the ENR in 1877.

The Eastern and Midlands Railway (later to become part of the M&GN) obtained an Act to build a branch line from North Walsham Town to a terminus at Mundesley but had to abandon the scheme in 1892 for lack of finance. However, after a period of in-fighting between inpecunious companies over rival territory, the purchase of the E&MR by the Midland Railway and the Great Northern Railway to combine into the M&GNR Joint Railway (1893) provided sounder finances. To this was added the strength of a take-over of the ENR by its parent GER management. In spite of arrangements of the E&MR takeover including the abandonment yet again of the Mundesley branch proposal, the first passenger train ran the 5½ miles from Mundesley to North Walsham on 1 July 1898. Since 1896, powers had been in hand to extend between Cromer and Mundesley but these were deferred until activity resumed in 1902. Differences of opinion as to land values caused much friction, so that actual building took until early 1903 to start. The Cromer to Mundesley extension finally opened for traffic on 3 August 1906 with both M&GNR and GER trains shown in the timetable. After the grouping the LNER and the successors to the M&GNR operated the line on a three-yearly, alternating basis. In spite of ideas to increase traffic including the opening of intermediate halts in the inter-war years, traffic declined to the extent that the section north of Mundesley closed completely on 17 April 1953 – whilst the remainder kept a passenger service until 5 October 1956 and freight until 28 December 1964.

Ex-LNER Class B12/3 4–6–0 No 61540 stands in front of Cromer Beach shed on 19 September 1954. With the closure of Cromer High station and its shed on 20 September 1954, all traffic was diverted to Cromer Beach (ex-M&GN) where the shed was transferred to the control of Norwich (32A) from being a sub-depot of Melton

Constable. On 26 September, 61540 was reported to be on shed along with B17s 61656/65/6 and N7 69690, motor fitted for working the Mundesley-on-Sea trains, though 61540 was also reported on this duty. *(J. Edgington)*

West Runton station looking towards Cromer, 1930s. A timber and corrugated iron station building is just out of view to the right. Opened with minimal goods facilities in September 1887, the station enjoyed plenty of passenger traffic in connection with the golf links adjoining the 'Links Hotel'. *(Lens of Sutton)*

Sheringham station, opened 16 June 1887, looking west in the 1920s with the fish loading dock siding on the left and Station Road level crossing behind the photographer. The footbridge was constructed along with improvements to the yard in 1896/7 when other alterations were made to the station buildings. The platforms were lengthened in 1907. The station was closed on 2 February 1967. *(Lens of Sutton)*

An M&GNR notice along with ex-LNER fire buckets still in existence at Weybourne station in September 1958. *(RAS Marketing)*

D13 class 4–4–0 No 8030 passes Wells-on-Sea Junction signalbox on 29 June 1936 with a train of vintage rolling stock from Dereham. The signals on the left mark the line of the Wells harbour branch. To the right is the West Norfolk Railway route to Heacham. *(H.C. Casserley)*

An example of a steel bodied 14 ton open wagon built by Charles Roberts & Co. Ltd of Wakefield in 1943 for the Wells-on-Sea firm of Claxton and Edwards. The design featured both an end opening door (denoted by the direction of the white stripe) and a side door. *(HMRS/C. Roberts Collection)*

Cromer Links Halt on the ex N&SJR route between Overstrand and Cromer Beach was opened in May 1923 by the LNER as part of a campaign to encourage more passenger traffic. This view looks towards Roughton Road Junction distant signal which has a concrete post. At the junction, the N&SJR was joined by the ex-GER line from Gunton. *(Lens of Sutton)*

M&GN Class A 4–4–2T No 9, built at Melton Constable in 1910, stands outside the engine shed at Cromer Beach, 27 September 1920. This locomotive was one in a class totalling only three. No 9 became LNER 09 and lasted in service until July 1944. *(LCGB/K. Nunn)*

Cromer Beach station looking towards the terminus with the train shed extending out over the platform. The train starting out towards Melton Constable under a somersault signal is one of the Johnson 0–4–4Ts on loan from the Midland Railway between 1906 and 1912. The engine shed and turntable are seen in the top left side. *(Lens of Sutton)*

Mundesley on Sea station looking north around the time of closure. The Eastern Region blue enamel station name has replaced an earlier M&GNR version but the M&GN style fencing remains intact. It opened to goods on 20 June 1898 and to passengers on 1 July 1898 when the local elementary school closed for the day, enabling the pupils to have their first experience of rail travel. The line onwards to Cromer was truncated on 6 April 1953 after which the sidings were used by holiday camping coaches. Final closure took place on 5 October 1964. (*D. Lawrence* per *H. Davies*)

County School station facing Wells, 1 September 1955. This station opened on 1 May 1882 as a result of the East Norfolk Railway extending the Wroxham branch to the Wells and Dereham line. Up and Down platforms were provided along with a bay for Wroxham services. The Norfolk County School was to the east of the station and became a naval training school, part of Dr Barnardo's Homes, in Edwardian times. (*R.M. Casserley*)

Ex-LNER Class B12/3 No 61568 on the 5.20 pm from Cromer approaching Wroxham station on 12 May 1953.

Cromer Yard signalbox in July 1964. Situated at the Melton Constable end of the platform, this box replaced a tall timber Eastern and Midlands Railway in about 1920. The cabin is noteworthy for being constructed using concrete (a material much favoured on the M&GNR) in the form of blocks and dressings. *(J. Edgington)*

Mundesley on Sea station from the forecourt, 31 March 1956. It incorporates mock Tudor of the Arts and Craft style. The importance attached to the architecture did not find expression in the station's traffic figures. The firm of Cornish and Gaymer of North Walsham, well known church restorers in the region, were responsible for the building contract. *(J. Edgington)*

Another view of GER T26 2–4–0 No 441 at Cromer standing just beyond the end of the station platform. *(HMRS/R. Hilton)*

Worstead station looking south, *c.* 1900. The train crew are accepting the token to allow the train to continue over the single line to Cromer. The locomotive is a GER Class D27 2–2–2, one of six converted to oil firing in 1896. *(HMRS/Hilton)*

Aylsham station Down Home signal on 8 October 1960. The station had 'South' added to its name from September 1948. The MacKenzie and Holland signal box along with the station can be glimpsed beyond. *(B.P. Hoper Collection)*

A large gathering at the northern end of North Walsham station offering few clues as to its occasion. The station canopy and half-timbered gables date from 1897/8 and the footbridge is of steel construction, put up as a replacement in 1910. The locomotive, M&GN No 28, is a Beyer, Peacock & Co Ltd Class A 4–4–0 delivered to the Eastern and Midlands Railway in 1883 and subsequently modified by the M&GN. *(Lens of Sutton)*

Briningham Single Line Junction on the Holt side of Melton Constable, 25 January 1964. The line from Melton Constable to Holt opened on 1 October 1884 as a single line, with the section from Melton to Briningham being doubled in June 1900 thereby requiring the box seen here to be opened. The vertical boarding construction looks to have more GNR influence in its design, in contrast to the more usually adopted MR style. *(B.P. Hoper Collection)*

M&GN Preservation Society special at Reepham station, 8 October 1960. The line opened from Wroxham to Reepham on 2 May 1881 and closed to passengers in September 1952. Goods traffic survived until 6 June 1981. The locomotive is ex-LNER Class B12 4–4–0 61572, now preserved. *(B.P. Hoper Collection)*

Cromer Beach station forecourt, 7 September 1968. Arts and Craft style again is utilised. Opening of the line from Mundesley to Cromer, built by the M&GNR, took place in 1906. The re-arrangement of operations which closed Cromer High station in 1954 resulted in diversion of all traffic into Cromer Beach station. (*Lens of Sutton*)

The initials of the Eastern and Midlands Railway are seen intertwined in the ornamental ironwork supporting the train shed at Cromer Beach station. The EMR was an amalgamation of the Lynn and Fakenham Railway with the Great Yarmouth and Stalham Light (sanctioned from 1 January 1883). The GN and MR jointly took over the E&MR from 1 July 1893 thereby rescuing it from receivership and making it part of the M&GNJR. *(Lens of Sutton)*

Edwardian elegance at Norwich: Great Eastern Railway's single driver Class P43 stands behind Norwich Goods Yard signalbox, *c.* 1900. The P43 Class were part of the GER'S experiment with oil burning apparatus, being the first type to be built in this form in 1898. *(HMRS/Hilton Collection)*

No 8030, a GER-built T19 class 4–4–0 subsequently rebuilt by the LNER and classified D13 takes water at Wells-on-Sea, 29 June 1936. The name was changed to Wells-next-the-Sea in 1957. The engine has probably just been turned on the 44 ft turntable that is in view. The tender faces in the direction of the two road engine shed. *(H.C. Casserley)*

Wells-next-the-Sea looking west with the former engine shed, by this date taken over by the goods department, 29 August 1960. The station stands to the left. It closed to passengers on 3 October 1964 and to freight from 31 October of the same year. *(R. Carpenter Collection)*

Dersingham station in 1911, looking north towards the main station building on the Up platform with the GER style canopy prominent. On the left, the timber signal box is a GER-type 7 design; whilst on the right beyond the cattle pens is an end loading dock with the only available goods store nearby in the form of a small, lock-up goods shed. *(HMRS/R. Hilton)*

Snettisham station looking north towards Hunstanton, 1911. The nearer of the two GER cattle vans is No 26080, built 1901. Above the other wagon in the distance (in the headshunt) is the gatekeeper's house. A substantial stone-built goods shed was available in Snettisham goods yard, the entrance to which is seen on the right where one of four sidings extended to Messrs Vynne and Everitt's granary. *(HMRS/R. Hilton)*

2

The East Norfolk Coast

The view from Station Road to the Italian style brick frontage of Norwich City station, *c.* 1910. Opened on 2 December 1882 as the terminal of a branch line from Melton Constable, it was authorised to the Lynn and Fakenham Railway but opened by the Eastern and Midlands Railway (E&MR) which subsequently became part of the M&GNR. In its heyday, a daily service to Birmingham was operated but the station closed to passengers in March 1959 and to goods until February 1969. *(Lens of Sutton)*

From Norwich to Great Yarmouth and the Coast

The original intention of the Eastern Counties Railway (authorized in 1836) was to link Norwich with London via Colchester, Ipswich and Diss but in the event only Colchester was reached. The continuation towards the East Anglian coast was completed by three other companies and it took them until 1849 to create a route through to Norwich with through running arrangements in place with other lines, but all on an uneasy and uncertain footing.

Meanwhile, the Yarmouth and Norwich Railway had been incorporated in June 1842 as the eastern, 20½ mile section of an east to west cross-country trunk route using the Yare Valley via Reedham. This route presented no major engineering problems for the company and was opened on 12 May 1844 with a daily service of four trains taking fifty minutes between termini. Access to Yarmouth across the River Bure was at first over a suspension bridge in private hands and adjacent to the Vauxhall Gardens, named after the famous London resort. (The Yarmouth and Norwich's terminal in Yarmouth was given the name Vauxhall in 1859 when the East Suffolk opened its Yarmouth station at South Town.)

The next railway development in the region was the Norwich and Brandon Railway which reached Norwich on 30 July 1845 having been delayed in awaiting the completion of the original Trowse Swing Bridge to allow the line to cross the River Wensum. In 1845 the Y&NR amalgamated to form the Norfolk Railway with the Norwich and Brandon Railway, which at Brandon met the Eastern Counties Railway extension of the Northern and Eastern Railway's route from London via Cambridge. The Eastern Union Railway's extension to Norwich was officially opened on 7 November 1849 joining the Brandon route at Trowse Lower Junction.

The other company to enter Norwich in this period was the Eastern Union Railway. Victoria station in Victoria Gardens by St Stephen's Gate provided their terminus in Norwich until 1854, when after a period of squabbling with the ECR, Thorpe station gained the position as the principal Norwich terminus. The whole of the ECR/EUR network eventually passed to the GER as part of the amalgamations of 1862. Thorpe station was rebuilt and enlarged in 1886, whilst, under legal prevention from closure to passengers by Norwich City corporation, City station kept a minimal passenger service until 1916. The station building was partly demolished in 1948 but the site played a significant role as a goods terminus until 1966.

Further development between Norwich and Yarmouth had occurred in 1847 when the Norwich–Reedham–Yarmouth line was joined by a route into Suffolk towards Lowestoft from Reedham worked by the Norfolk Railway.

The popularity of seaside holidays in late Victorian times led to Yarmouth's growth from an important fishing town to a seaside holiday destination as well; and, as this function grew, an 11 mile-long single line relief route, opened in 1883, shortened the distance from Norwich to the coast and introduced an alternative for the GER's coast-bound traffic. This relief line ran from Brundall via Acle to Breydon Junction to reach Yarmouth and thereby, importantly, also gave rail access for the Norfolk Broads – an additional part of the region's increasing attractions for summer visitors.

South Town was the second station in Yarmouth to accommodate trains over the East Suffolk Railway which joined the Eastern Union Railway at Woodbridge, the Yarmouth section splitting at Beccles. The ECR bought out the ESR and the line to South Town was opened on 1 June 1859.

The double track portion of line between Brundall and Reedham was extended from Norwich to Reedham in 1874, the year when a head-on collision between the Up mail train from Yarmouth and Lowestoft and the 5 pm London to Yarmouth express resulted in twenty-one fatalities.

Both routes from Yarmouth to Norwich were used at greatest intensity between the two World Wars when summer holiday traffic from the Midlands and the North as well as London was at its peak. However, developments of agricultural enterprises of any size were restricted to a sugar beet factory at Cantley, opened in 1912. When a collision occurred in 1983 between a coaster heading for this factory and the open span of Reedham swing bridge, the repair costs accrued were a major factor in bringing about the demise of the whole line, which thereby did not benefit from the revitalisation of the route via Acle that followed the closure of the rival ex-M&GNR network to Yarmouth (Beach) station in 1959.

Yarmouth (South Town) survived flooding in 1953, but was closed under BR in 1970 with the station buildings being demolished in 1977.

The M&GN Routes

In Norwich, the M&GN became responsible for operating the third terminus when they opened the City station on 2 December 1882. This line connected the North Norfolk coast via Melton Constable with regular operations and services to Birmingham, the North East and Lancashire. Originating through a scheme set up by the Lynn and Fakenham Railway Company, the opening of the line was completed later by the Eastern and Midlands Railway which had taken over the L&FR via an amalgamation.

Along with the rest of the M&GN system, City station became an early casualty for passengers in the Beeching era, closing to them on 2 March 1959. The freight side of the system was kept on, however, until 3 February 1969.

In Yarmouth, the Great Yarmouth and Stalham Light Railway opened on 7 August 1877. This created the need for the construction of another terminus (later to become Beach station) in the town, being separated from Vauxhall and Southtown by the Rivers Bure and Yare. Extension to North Walsham from Stalham brought about a change of company name to the Yarmouth and North Norfolk (Y&NN) in 1881. Yarmouth's connection via North Walsham and Melton Constable with the Midlands and North through its Beach station was invaluable to its rise as a holiday resort – let alone the important freight traffic, some of it via the Yarmouth Union Railway which opened between Beach station and North Quay in May 1882, with a junction to the GER'S tramway system in the port.

The Y&NN amalgamated with the Lynn and Fakenham Railway to become the Eastern and Midlands Railway, creating a route via the Great Northern Railway at Spalding and Peterborough so that excursions from Yorkshire arrived at the Beach station; and special fares were offered from London (Kings Cross) to Yarmouth (Beach).

The GNR connection was later to be enhanced when in 1893 the EMR became part of the take over by the M&GNR.

A link was made north of Yarmouth Beach station over the 800 ft swing bridge across Breydon Water, the largest engineering work on the M&GNR, to the Norfolk and Suffolk Joint Railway's route south from Yarmouth (South Town) to Lowestoft, the fifth and final line to serve Great Yarmouth. The Act for a direct line from South Town to Lowestoft was obtained by the GER in 1897 and the line became part of the N&SJR the following year. The Norfolk and Suffolk Railway Joint Committee was an example of co-operation between the GER and M&GNR in 1898 and opened its link, just over 9 miles long, between Yarmouth (South Town) and Lowestoft on 13 July 1903, lasting as a railway route until final closure on 4 May 1970.

Riddles BR Britannia Class 4–6–2 No 70006 *Robert Burns* of Norwich shed (32A) stands at Norwich, Thorpe on 20 February 1959 with a rake of standard BR carriages, by this date in maroon livery. *(B.P. Hoper Collection)*

On a typical duty for a locomotive of its type at the time, 4MT 2–6–0 No 43145 stands in Yarmouth Beach station surrounded by steam in February 1959. This class was an Ivatt design with a taper boiler introduced by the LMS in 1947. *(B. Wilson, courtesy B.P. Hoper)*

The footplate crew pose in the cab of BR Britannia Class 4–6–2 No 70006 *Robert Burns* whilst it stands at Norwich, soon after introduction to Great Eastern main line duties in May 1951. The double white discs on the buffer beam signify the locomotive is ready to work an express train. The engine does not yet carry a shedplate on its smokebox door but had a long association with BR shed 32A (Norwich). *(LCGB/K. Nunn)*

Ex-LNER Class D16/3 4–4–0 No 62586 heads the 4.45 pm from Yarmouth Vauxhall into Norwich Thorpe, 17 July 1954. A Class L1 2–6–4T stands beyond the signal box whilst the engine shed's giant coaling tower dating from 1936 stands out against the skyline to the right above the roof of the signal box. *(Philip Kelley)*

'The East Anglian', the 11.40 am for Liverpool Street, leaves Norwich headed by Class B1 4–6–0 No 61040 *Roedeer*. This locomotive was the first of its class delivered to the LNER from the outside contractors, North British Railway Company, in April 1946. No 61040 was withdrawn in July 1966. *(LCGB/K. Nunn)*

Class F3 2–4–2T No 8045 and No 8062 at Norwich, 30 June 1936. The F3 was a J. Holden design introduced on the GER as class C32 between 1895 and 1902, a tank engine version of the E4 'Intermediate' class. They were a popular choice for rural branch line duties and some of the class survived long enough to come into BR ownership. No 8045 was withdrawn from Norwich shed in August 1947. *(H.C Casserley)*

BR Britannia class 4–6–2 70006 *Robert Burns* of Norwich shed works hard around the curve through Wensum in April 1961. By this date, only two ex-LNER carriages are marshalled in the train otherwise consisting of standard BR Mark 1 stock in maroon livery. *(P.H. Groom)*

A somewhat begrimed BR Britannia class 4–6–2 70005 *John Milton* pulls away from Norwich with the 'East Anglian' express for Liverpool Street station, early 1950s, when the train consisted of ex-LNER Gresley carriage stock in crimson and cream livery. Ex-GER signal posts dominate the scene and a vintage clerestory roofed carriage is in the foreground. *(P.H. Groom)*

Ex-LNER Class B12/3 4–6–0 No 61514 of Norwich shed at Norwich Thorpe, 18 June 1957, on the 1.35 pm Norwich to Cromer, passes an ex-LNER upper quadrant signal on a short post contrasting with the tall ex-GER signalposts in the background. Signs pointing to the demise of steam in the region are seen in the refuelling pipes and the diesel multiple units alongside the steam-hauled train. *(B. Wilson, courtesy B.P. Hoper)*

The Breydon Swing Bridge and viaduct across Breydon Water looking from the south west bank towards Yarmouth, 1 October 1955. Designed by William Marriot and his assistant in 1899 the bridge was opened in 1903 at a cost of £63,131 6*s* 2*d*. The swing span was 169 ft 8 in, pivoted on a central ball bearing and rollers on a circular path powered by an 11 h.p. gas engine. The control was from a cabin above the swing section whilst a signal box at either end controlled the single track line. Habitually kept open for the passage of river traffic, the bridge closed to trains in 1953 and was demolished in 1962. *(LCGB/K. Nunn)*

LNER Class B12/1 4–6–0 No 8562 stands at Norwich on 30 June 1936 apparently in the attractive LNER livery of apple green with black and white lining with shaded gold lettering. Derived from the GER Holden class S69, these locos were entrusted with hauling the principal expresses in Norfolk in the 1920s and '30s. They were judged to be one of the UK's most successful inside cylinder 4–6–0 design locomotives and yet were the subject of several redesigns by Sir Nigel Gresley, including the fitting of a larger diameter, round topped boiler. No 8562 was the last of the class to be dealt with in this way in 1938. *(H.C. Casserley)*

L N E R
8814

With footplatemen in the cab, LNER Class D16/3 No 8814 at Norwich, 30 June 1936, stands in line with a Class J15 0–6–0. Rebuilt with a round topped boiler from a GER Class D15 that was built in 1910, 8814 lasted in service until BR days, being withdrawn in April 1955. *(H.C. Casserley)*

LNER class E4 2–4–0 No 7485 stands at Norwich on 30 June 1936 displaying the post-1927 LNER livery and the cast-iron-lipped chimney that replaced the earlier Holden GER class T26 stovepipe version from *c.* 1930. Built in November 1894, this engine did not last as long as some of its fellow members, being withdrawn in January 1940. *(H.C. Casserley)*

LNER class E4 2–4–0 No 7407 stands 'dead' at Norwich with its smokebox door open for servicing, 30 June 1936. This locomotive, built in 1902, lasted well into BR days and was only withdrawn in June 1956 as BR No 62792, having been allocated to Norwich shed as late as June 1955. *(H.C. Casserley)*

Norwich Victoria station viewed across the forecourt with the train sheds visible on the left and right, *c.* 1910. The Eastern Union Railway acquired Victoria Gardens as the site for its Norwich terminus in readiness for the opening of the line in 1849. The platforms were laid out in a 'V' shape with an ornamental garden infilling the gap. The station went into decline with the opening of the Trowse Junctions (North and South) in 1851 with most passenger traffic then operating from Norwich Thorpe. Victoria retained passenger services until May 1916 but kept a goods department until after the Second World War when the buildings began to be demolished, starting in 1948. From January 1966, coal traffic only remained and even that disappeared in 1986 leaving the site for redevelopment. (*Stations UK*)

A view looking through to the portico of the main Norwich (City) station building, *c.* 1890, with a dumb buffered wagon amongst those in the sidings alongside Ruymp and Son's building materials site. There were four station platform faces but the two centre lines were mainly for stock storage. The two main awnings were supported on spandrels bearing the E&MR insignia. *(Lens of Sutton)*

M & GN
POTTER HEIGHAM BRIDGE HAL
PROPOSED BUS TIMETABLES
MELTON CONSTABLE TO
YARMOUTH BEACH

Belton station looking from the signalbox towards Yarmouth with the Up platform on the right hand side, 12 October 1911. Goods and coalyard sidings are in the distance. *(HMRS/R. Hilton Collection)*

Opposite, above: Stalham looking in the direction of Yarmouth, 1920s. Opened in 1880 when the nameboard read Stalham (for Happisburgh and Palling on Sea). In view is the MR type signalbox of *c.* 1907 on the Up platform along with an E&MR lifting water crane, a timber waiting shelter and a concrete block hut. Goods facilities included a shed, end loading dock and cattle pens. In addition to providing a railhead for boating holidaymakers, much of the local blackcurrant harvest was despatched by train prior to line closure in February 1959. *(Lens of Sutton)*

Opposite, below: The minute Potter Heigham Bridge Halt was opened in 1933 to offer a passenger train platform for the nearby Broadland holiday market which was by this period growing at a rapid rate. *(Lens of Sutton)*

BOLSOVER

Norwich Thorpe station opened in 1886. This view on 1 June 1914 shows 6-wheeled carriage stock standing in the terminus alongside two of five platforms in use at the time. Behind the platform canopies can be seen part of the station concourse and, further away, the large dome surmounting the main building can be partly seen. *(R. Carpenter Collection)*

Opposite, above: A second view of Belton taken from the Down starter signal and looking towards London, 12 October 1911. The vehicle at the far end of the siding is a GNR 6-wheel van with a high-sided GER open wagon loaded with sacks next to it. The horse and cart is well in evidence as the prime means of further distribution. *(HMRS/R. Hilton Collection)*

Opposite, below: A Wickham and Co petrol driven trolley and trailer in use by the Permanent Way gang stands at Reedham looking east, mid-1950s, with Reedham Junction signal box out of view opposite the bracket signal with a concrete post. *(C. Maggs)*

80

Yarmouth Beach station where M&GN class C 4–4–0 No 78 gently simmers after bringing its train into the terminus platform that ran parallel to Nelson Road. No 78 was supplied by Beyer, Peacock and Co in 1899. *(H.C. Casserley)*

Opposite, above: M&GN class C 4–4–0 No 80, the last in the series to be delivered from Beyer, Peacock and Co, leaves Norwich City station on 26 June 1929. To the left are the locomotive sheds with the water tank and mess room in view. *(H.C. Casserley)*

Opposite, below: The somersault signal at Norwich City station permits the departure of the 5.20 pm to Melton Constable on 26 June 1929. The track behind the signal is connected to the shed turntable and beyond is the River Wensum which appears to be in flood. The locomotive is M&GN class C 4–4–0 No 80. *(H.C. Casserley)*

Class P43 4–2–2 No 14 departing from Norwich Thorpe, *c.* 1905, whilst a shunting signal allows a tank engine and train to proceed from the adjacent platform. Little is seen of the sleepers in the track which is heavily

ballasted in a manner typical of the period. To the right is a GER mail van, complete with bag catching apparatus, coupled to a ventilated milk van. *(HMRS/R. Hilton Collection)*

Yarmouth Vauxhall station, 9 June 1954, and the 2 pm from Norwich has brought a good contingent of passengers with it. Ex-LNER Class D16/3 4–4–0 No 62510 of Norwich shed has hauled the stopping train. The cast-iron pillars and roof supports were identical to those designed by Samuel Morton Peto and Thomas Grissell for the original Norwich Thorpe terminus. *(J. Edgington)*

A view from Yarmouth Vauxhall station signalbox looking beneath the M&GN line towards Norwich, 26 September 1911. The scissors crossover towards the centre of the picture marks the running line to Breydon Junction. *(HMRS/R. Hilton Collection)*

A Thornycroft J class single deck bus outside Norwich Thorpe station, *c.* 1920, just before the GER bus service was taken over. The service started in 1905 from Trowse station, moving to Victoria station then diverting to Thorpe when Victoria closed. Behind the bus can be seen a little of the stone and brick facade of W. Ashbee's design for the 1886 station rebuilding. *(Norfolk Railway Society* per *M. Fordham)*

Ex-LNER Class D16/3 4–4–0 No 62577 waits to depart from Norwich Thorpe on a stopping train, August 1955. Ex-GER carriage stock is still in evidence behind the loco which was withdrawn from Norwich shed in October 1956. *(RAS/Photomatic)*

Yarmouth South Town viewed from beyond the station signalbox looking towards London and the GER engine shed, 26 September 1911. A GER Class Y 14 0–6–0 waits by the water crane and ash disposal point. A set of shearlegs for lifting heavy loads is visible above the shed roof and the productive allotment on the right no doubt supplemented the railwaymen's wages. *(HMRS/R. Hilton)*

Yarmouth Vauxhall station with diesel motive power as station pilot, 8 June 1954. Drewry Car Co Ltd, diesel mechanical 0–6–0 No 11103 of Yarmouth Vauxhall shed (32E) was introduced in 1952 to replace the ex-GER Tram engines. Ex-LNER Class D16/3 4–4–0 No 62586 awaits departure on the 1.50 pm train to Norwich. *(J. Edgington)*

Ex-LNER Class B17/2 4–6–0 No 61612 *Houghton Hall* stands at Norwich shed with a full load of coal in its ex-GER tender awaiting its next turn of duty on 12 July 1959, just two months before withdrawal. The Sandringham 4–6–0s had been the mainstay of Norfolk expresses for many years but the class had been decimated in numbers by the date of this photograph. *(J. Edgington)*

Ex-LNER B17/2 4–6–0 No 61638 *Melton Hall* leaves Norwich Thorpe with the 1.40 pm Yarmouth train on 2 September 1951. The leading carriage is an ex-SR continental traffic vehicle including a 2nd Class compartment peculiar to that service. *(Philip Kelley)*

C E
30469

444
C E

GER Class S46 4–4–0 No 1886 crossing the River Wensum over the original Trowse Swing Bridge heading south *c*.1905. The signalbox is visible in the background. The bridge was constructed to the design of G.P. Bidder and opened in 1845. The bridge provided the link between the Brandon and Norwich Railway and the Norfolk Railway's terminus at Thorpe. It was rebuilt in 1906 and again in 1986. *(HMRS/R. Hilton Collection)*

Opposite, above: Norwich, *c*. June 1911, the year the GER ventilated van in the photograph was built. The siding is at the eastern end of the locomotive depot and Carrow Road is in the background. It is the time of the Royal Agricultural Show and the bell tents are part of the arrangements, as is the whitewashed barrel. (Perhaps the van has also been treated in this fashion?) *(HMRS/R. Hilton Collection)*

Opposite, below: The tender of GER Class T26 2–4–0 No 444 has come to grief at Crown Point sidings, Norwich during the Royal Agricultural Show in June 1911. The GER were stretched to the limit with special trains during the four days of the show which included a visit from HM King George V. *(HMRS/R. Hilton Collection)*

Trowse swingbridge with a No 1 Class 2–4–0 heading a Dereham via Wymondham train, *c.* 1905. The iron castings were made and assembled at Regent's Canal Ironworks and transported on barges via the coast to Norwich. *(HMRS/R. Hilton collection)*

Opposite, above: A burnished Johnson 'Little Sharpie', GER Class No 1 2–4–0 No 49 stands near the Goods Yard signalbox at Norwich, *c.* 1905. *(HMRS/R. Hilton Collection)*

Opposite, below: View taken from Trowse Swing Bridge signal box looking north towards Thorpe station with the Wensum curve bearing off to the right towards Whitlingham Junction. This curve opened in 1879 and eradicated a reversal at Norwich Thorpe by trains from Thetford or Ipswich. A temporary platform can be seen situated on the Wensum curve in connection with The Royal Agricultural Show, which was in full swing when the photograph was taken on 30 June 1911. *(HMRS/R. Hilton Collection)*

Looking towards Norwich Thorpe station from the Carrow Road overbridge on a dull October day in 1911. The station signalbox is in view under the signal gantry. The engine shed to the left is full of GER locomotives whilst loco coal is ready for final delivery in company wagons. To the right is a line of horse boxes and nearest the camera two carriage trucks on which would have been loaded horse drawn conveyances. *(HMRS/R. Hilton Collection)*

Opposite, above: During April and May 1949, extensive trials were run on the GE section of BR with ex-SR Bulleid Battle of Britain Class 4–6–2 No 34059 *Sir Archibald Sinclair* seen here at Norwich on 18 May 1949 about to start the Up 'Norfolkman' express to Liverpool Street station. The trials contributed to an evaluation of the proposed Britannia Class 4–6–2s that were later introduced. Alongside is ex-LNER Class D16/3 No 62581 on the 10.40 am York–Lowestoft. *(LCGB/K. Nunn)*

Opposite, below: LNER Clayton and Co Ltd steam railcar No 43302 *Chevy Chase* approaches Norwich on the 4.26 pm from Lowestoft, 2 May 1931. *(LCGB/K. Nunn)*

Constructed in 1896 by Neilson and Co to the design of Johnson's MR Class 2284, M&GN Class D No 64 stands outside Yarmouth Beach shed on 29 June 1914. *(LCGB/K. Nunn)*

Opposite, above: A privately owned, 14-ton tank wagon built by Charles Roberts and Co in 1927. *(HMRS/C. Roberts Collection)*

Opposite, below: Temporary platforms were set up by the GER at Crown Point Sidings, Norwich to accommodate traffic for the Royal Agricultural Show in 1911. Horse boxes and a carriage truck of 1886 vintage comprise the rolling stock. *(HMRS/R. Hilton Collection)*

E & D. STOKES
ROYAL INSURANCE BUILDINGS
No. 1. NORWICH
9-2-0
E & D STOKES
ROYAL INSURANCE BUILDINGS
No 1 NORWICH

G E 142

67199
C1

62037

GER Class G16 4–4–0 No 0704 at Yarmouth *c.* 1900. The G16 was one of five new locomotive types introduced in the three and a half years following the appointment of T.W. Worsdell as Locomotive Superintendent of the GER in 1882. The class were the subject of mechanical experimentation when first introduced and had been rebuilt by the time of this view. This class was one of the first to appear in GER Royal Blue livery. *(LCGB/K. Nunn Collection)*

pposite, above: Yarmouth South Town station, looking towards the station concourse and the malthouse longside High Mill Road, 8 June 1954. South Town was the terminus of the East Suffolk Railway from Ipswich pened throughout on 1 June 1859. Ex-LNER Class F5 2–4–2T 67199 of South Town shed (32D) has arrived on he 12.34 pm Beccles to Yarmouth push and pull unit. *(J. Edgington)*

pposite, below: Class K1 2–6–0 No 62037 uses the turntable to the south of Yarmouth South Town station ooking north on 4 February 1959. 62037 like most of the K1s in East Anglia spent most of its years at ambridge shed (31B). These mixed traffic engines were developed by A.H. Peppercorn from the earlier . Thompson Class K1/1 2–6–0s. *(J. Edgington)*

1006

'lass K3/2 2–6–0 No 61817 of Stratford shed at Yarmouth Vauxhall station looking towards the bufferstops with he goods shed roof to the right, 24 September 1952. Vauxhall station opened on 1 May 1884 and was rebuilt by .961. The K3s were a Gresley design and were originally transferred in small numbers to the GE section in 1938 rom ex-GNR sheds. *(D. Lawrence, courtesy H. Davies)*

pposite, above: Holden Class D27 2–2–2 No 1006 seen at Norwich on 3 November 1895. In the following year o 1006 was one of six of its class to be used for the experimental fitting of oil firing equipment for use on romer expresses. The lighter mainline express trains at the turn of the century were still being hauled by this ass of engine. *(LCGB/K. Nunn)*

pposite, below: Yarmouth Vauxhall shed, July 1955, looking south with the turntable just out of picture to the ght. Given shed code 32E in the Norwich district by BR, the two-road shed dating from 1883 is being occupied y two D16/3 locomotives. The leading one, 62613, is one of six of the class allocated to Vauxhall shed at the me. *(R. Carpenter Collection)*

Ex-LNER Holden Class E4 2–4–0 No 62787 at Norwich Thorpe Junction heading towards Norwich, 18 June 1952. Thorpe junction signalbox is just out of shot to the right and the London lines are in the foreground. Built in 1895, this engine was not withdrawn until November 1956. *(L.R. Peters, courtesy Gresley Society Collection)*

Opposite, above: Built by Sharp, Stewart and Co., Johnson GER Class No 1, 'Little Sharpie', 2–4–0 No 48 waits at Norwich Thorpe with the 6.17 pm train to Wells on 11 June 1909. W. Ashbee's dome design in the background contrasts with the plain style of the platform area of the station. *(LCGB/K. Nunn Collection)*

Opposite, below: A Railway Correspondence and Travel Club special visits Norwich Victoria on 31 March 1962. Diesel Mechanical 0–6–0 No 11168 has provided the motive power on this stage of the trip. The sidings at Victoria played a major part in handling freight traffic in Norwich. *(J. Edgington)*

The LNER's publicity department organised a number of displays at sites around the railway to show the public the latest LNER rolling stock. On 2 May 1931 Sir Nigel Gresley's experimental high pressure 4-cylinder compound with water tube boiler was on display at Norwich. With a wheel arrangement of 4–6–4, No 10000 was later rebuilt in a more conventional form with a streamlined casing similar to the A4 4–6–2s to be numbered by BR as 60700. *(LCGB/K. Nunn Collection)*

Ex-LNER D16/3 No 62586 4–4–0 at Yarmouth Vauxhall shed, 29 September 1953. This building replaced an earlier locomotive shed to the north of the station. A clerestory coach survives in departmental use. *(F.A. Wycherley)*

LNER Class Y10 No 8187 on the quayside at Great Yarmouth, 25 June 1947. Two Y10 class engines were built for the LNER by the Sentinel Loco Company in 1930 intended for the Wisbech and Upwell Tramway. To satisfy the requirements of the Tramway they had side valances, animal guards and double ended cabs. They were not a success and were soon transferred to Yarmouth for shunting the quayside lines. No 8187 was scrapped in August 1948 with the second loco lasting until 1952. *(F.A. Wycherley)*

M&GN Class C 4–4–0 No 38 about to depart from Norwich City station on 30 June 1936 with the 7.18 pm train to Melton Constable. *(H.C. Casserley)*

LNER Class J65 0–6–0T No 8215 crosses Yarmouth Vauxhall Bridge, 1 September 1948. The bridge in the photograph was a replacement of the original suspension bridge which was in the private ownership of a Mr Cory. In 1845 as a result of a freak accident the bridge collapsed with the loss of seventy-nine lives. *(LCGB/K. Nunn)*

Opposite: Progress was naturally slow for Drewry Diesel Mechanical BR No 11111 along the street section o track on North Quay, Great Yarmouth, 24 September 1952. Garson Blake and Co Ltd's lorry appears to be parkec across the running line (below). *(Both photos D. Lawrence,* per *H. Davies)*

BLAKE & SON
SLATING
& TILING
PET STORES
JCT 329

CARSON BLAKE & SON
SLATING
& TILING
CULLAMIX

GER Sinclair Class Y 2–4–0 stands at Norwich, *c.* 1890. Introduced in 1859 by Robert Sinclair for the Eastern Counties Railway, in 1865, because of excessive demand on British manufacturers, the GER went to Schneider et Cie of le Creusot, France to order fifteen of this class and fifteen Class W 2–2–2s. *(LCGB/K Nunn Collection)*

Opposite, above: BR Drewry DM 0–6–0 No 1103 shunts at Great Yarmouth Quayside on 24 September 1952 shortly after being delivered ex-works to Yarmouth Vauxhall shed (32E). Fully enclosed working parts below the footplate (side valances) plus a 'cow catcher' (animal guard) below the buffer beam made these locomotives safer in order to work along the public highway. This was a requirement of the Yarmouth Union Railway Act of 1880 for any locomotive working along the Yarmouth Tramway. No 11103 later became BR Class 04 No D2203. *(T.G. Wassell* per *H. Davies)*

Opposite, below: No 1 Class 2–4–0 'Little Sharpie' No 0105 stands in Norwich shed yard, 17 September 1910. The 4-wheeled tender is noteworthy. *(LCGB/K. Nunn Collection)*

11103

Norwich shed yard from Carrow Road, 1950s, showing developments compared with the view in 1911. The concrete coaling tower now dominates the scene. *(R. Carpenter Collection)*

Opposite, above: Haddiscoe yard on the Reedham and Lowestoft Branch, looking towards Reedham, with Haddiscoe Yard signalbox on the left in the distance, 26 September 1911. Haddiscoe station on the left was disused, having been closed since 1904. The Queen's Head public house is seen the other side of the New Cut waterway by the lifting bridge. *(HMRS/R. Hilton Collection)*

Opposite, below: A coal merchant's truck from the ex-Norfolk and Suffolk Railway route built by Charles Roberts and Co Ltd, Wakefield, 1933 and registered by the LNER. *(HMRS/C. Roberts Collection)*

B. RAYWOOD & SONS
COAL
MERCHANTS
No. 1933.
GORLESTON-ON-SEA
TARE 6-19-0
LOAD 12 TONS
2602

61659
61659

26

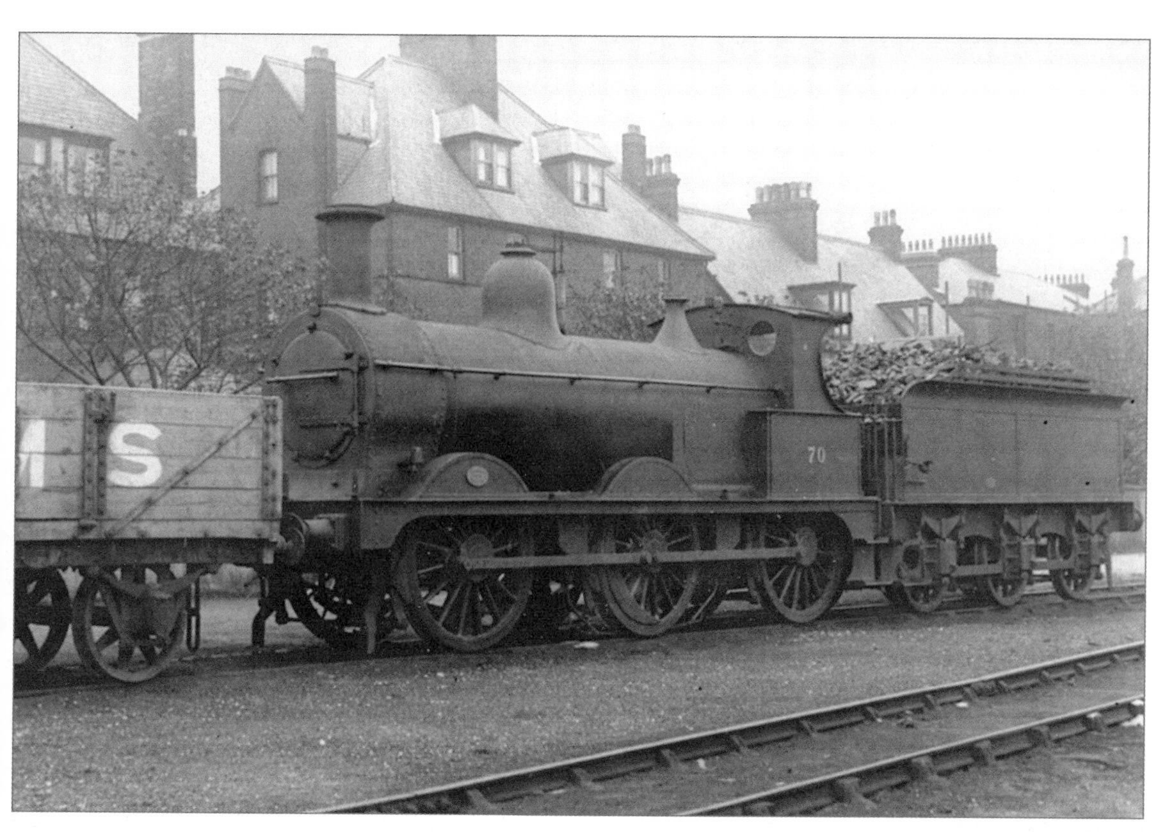

M&GN Class D 0–6–0 No 70 at Yarmouth Beach *c.* 1932. Built by Kitson & Co. in 1899 and later allocated an LNER number which it never carried, No 70 was withdrawn in 1944. *(Lens of Sutton, courtesy M&GN Circle)*

Opposite, above: Yarmouth South Town shed (32D) looking north, *c.* 1953. The shed fabric has reached a decrepit condition and the roof has collapsed or been demolished. A corrugated shelter has been positioned over one road and in 1957/8 a new shed building replaced the old. The Sandringham Class B17 No 61659 *East Anglian* had its streamlining removed in 1951 and was employed from South Town shed on Yarmouth to London expresses between 1953 and 1959. *(R. Carpenter Collection)*

Opposite, below: Eastern and Midlands Railway No 26 in original condition at Great Yarmouth station mid-1880s. These Class A locomotives were supplied by Messrs Beyer, Peacock and Co of Manchester and were painted chocolate, lined in black and chrome yellow. *(John D. Horan Collection, courtesy M&GN Circle)*

Yarmouth Beach shed turntable, *c.* 1928. M&GN Class C 4–4–0 No 48 is fully coaled up for its next duty. This locomotive has been fitted with an extended smokebox. *(Lens of Sutton, courtesy M&GN Circle)*

A group of M&GN staff based at the offices in Austin Street, Lynn enjoy an outing to Potter Heigham, 1925. *(A.A. Francis, W.C. Tuck Collection, courtesy M&GN Circle)*

Filling in for male employees away at the war, women were employed by the M&GN at the King's Lynn Austin Street offices from 1915. Here in 1917 are M&GN office staff, from left to right, Misses Sparkes, Fitzgerald, Hall, Heseltine, Hayes, van Loey and Freeman. *(Gerald Hayes, courtesy M&GN Circle)*

The staff plus one addition at Gayton Road station, *c.* 1904 (see following chapter). The pillbox cap of the staff member holding the little girl denotes his status as a stationmaster whereas manual staff dressed in green corduroy at the time. *(W.C. Tuck Collection, courtesy M&GN Circle)*

3

West Norfolk

The neat and tidy Wolferton station looking towards Hunstanton, 1921. Slightly over 6 miles from King's Lynn, the station had Tudor-style buildings on both platforms which were built for a total cost of £8,132 in 1898. A small clock tower was incorporated into the Up platform architecture, while the Down side Royal waiting rooms included oak panelled retiring rooms furnished with couches and easy chairs. Wolferton station was closely associated with Sandringham estate which provided much traffic, farm produce out, coal in, but was never particularly busy with local passengers. In BR(E) days, the stationmaster was Edmund Skillings, signalmen included Mr Green, Jack Harper and Aubrey Reddington whilst Mr Clemshaw, Mr Cox and George Bayfield were employed at Wolferton during this period. *(RAS Marketing)*

King's Lynn to Hunstanton

The Lynn and Hunstanton Railway was incorporated in 1861 and opened its 15 mile-long single line branch on 3 October 1862.

The L&HR shared some directors with the East Anglian Railways (later to become a part of the GER) from which it was independent in name only. A purpose built holiday village named New Hunstanton was part of the overall plan to develop Hunstanton; then, when HRH the Prince of Wales purchased the Sandringham estate in 1862, the line was suddenly elevated in status through its association with royal trains.

In 1874, the L&HR merged with the West Norfolk Junction Railway from Heacham to form the Hunstanton and West Norfolk which was absorbed by the Great Eastern Railway on 1 July 1890. The 6½ miles route from Kings Lynn to Wolferton was doubled by 1898, with Wolferton station being rebuilt at the same time, improvements made to passenger facilities and the signalling modernised.

By the time the LNER was formed in 1922, the introduction of holidays with pay gave a boost to the popularity of seaside resorts, The luxurious nature of the train service can be exemplified by the 8.30 am departure from Liverpool Street to Hunstanton, which ran with both an ordinary restaurant car and Pullman car accommodation.

In an attempt to regain the pre-war popularity of the line, a weekday express leaving Liverpool Street station for Hunstanton was named the 'Fenman' in 1949 but after the closure of the M&GN lines to the west in 1959, the rail connection from the Midlands

Wolferton looking north east, *c.* 1911. This was the main connecting station for the royal estate at Sandringham, hence the buffer stop and even the point rodding have been painted white! The building on the right with a ventilated belfry is a small gas works which supplied the station lamps. The running line is on the right and from here on was single track to Hunstanton. *(HMRS/R. Hilton Collection)*

came as a blow to traffic numbers. Freight services were withdrawn in 1964, whilst a minimal passenger service struggled to exist until 3 May 1969.

The West Norfolk Railway

Although in theory an independent company, the West Norfolk Railway was under the direction of the Lynn and Hunstanton Railway from its inception. Encouraged by the initial success in developing Hunstanton by means of rail connection, the WNR sought and gained Parliamentary approval on 23 June 1864. With backing from the GER as well as the L&HR, a route was relatively easily established from Heacham to Wells-next-the-Sea.

The engineer, J.H. Valentine, constructed a line using light railway principles of economy as instructed by the promoters, so that the intermediate stations such as Stanhoe and Holkham were given only basic facilities of one platform, without any goods sidings.

Although failing its first Board of Trade inspection, the railway did finally open on 17 August 1866. Previously there had been rumours of an unofficial royal outing by train from Sandringham to Holkham Hall. Income failed to come up to anticipation over the initial trading period and consequently a merger of the WNR with the L&HR was established – the title of the new company being the Hunstanton and West Norfolk Railway from 8 June 1878, an arrangement which lasted until the H&WNR was sold to the GER in 1890.

In LNER years, between the two World Wars, excursion traffic particularly from the Midlands kept income buoyant and the LNER were encouraged to implement improved facilities at the stations, especially at Heacham.

The Wells to Heacham line lasted with a regular passenger timetable only until 31 May 1952, and then suffered destruction between Wells and Holkham at the time of the disastrous floods of January 1953. Only the 11 mile length between Heacham and Burnham Market retained a freight service until 1964.

The Lynn and Ely Railway

The Lynn and Ely Railway, later East Anglian Railways, from Lynn (later King's Lynn) opened to Downham Market on 27 October 1846 and to Denver Road Gate in January 1847 against a background of financial difficulties. These were partly the result of engineering problems experienced in building the chosen route across marshy fenland with intervening river crossings. Suffering from grave financial troubles, East Anglian Railways was taken over by the Eastern Counties Railway on 1 January 1852 after disputes with the Great Northern Railway relating to running powers had been settled in court. The ECR was subsequently absorbed by the GER in 1862.

Other lines were opened to Hunstanton, Sutton Bridge and towards Fakenham, with mergers leading to the formation of the Midland and Eastern (1866) and the Eastern and Midlands (1883). These in turn merged into the Midland and Great Northern Joint Railway with its control centre situated at Lynn (re-named King's Lynn after 1911).

A replacement station was built as a jointly funded development by the GNR, GER and MR. Much later, after the LNER had succeeded to ownership of the King's Lynn station, a further rebuilding took place in 1938.

The railway system at Lynn was completed by systems extending to the harbour and then to the quays, with the opening of a swing bridge over the River Nar. In addition, a docks branch completed the link by rail with shipping transport.

One of the ornate platform lamps at Wolferton station decorated with miniature crowns. A story is told of a visiting circus elephant being tethered to one of these lamp-posts whilst the other animals were being unloaded. In an attempt to free itself, the elephant proceeded to uproot the lamp-post completely! *(Lens of Sutton)*

THE STOKE FERRY BRANCH

At Denver a line branched off through Ryston and Abbey to form the Stoke Ferry Branch. Built by an independent company and promoted by local landowners and gentry, the branch opened for all traffic on 1 August 1882 under GER management and was absorbed by that company on 15 July 1897. Passenger trains operated from Downham Market to Stoke Ferry until 22 September 1930. In 1905 Abbey became the junction for the privately owned Wissington Light Railway which included, from 1924, traffic generated by a sugar beet factory and which enabled the Denver to Abbey exchange sidings to remain open until 1982.

The Lynn and Dereham Railway

The Lynn and Dereham Railway was part of an important link between West Norfolk and Norwich via Dereham and Wymondham. Formed by an Act of 21 July 1845, the Lynn and Dereham, Lynn and Ely and the Ely and Huntingdon railways were amalgamated to form the East Anglian Railways before becoming part of the GER in 1862. The L&DR route opened by stages to Narborough, Swaffham and finally to Dereham in 1848. Operated as a single line with passing places, King's Lynn to Dereham remained open until 7 September 1968.

WISBECH BRANCH AND THE WISBECH AND UPWELL TRAMWAY

The Wisbech branch, almost in its entirety in Norfolk, opened from Magdalen Road (named Watlington until 1875) in February 1848. It was a line built to block or prevent other rivals gaining access to King's Lynn rather than to tap potential traffic from the neighbourhood. The last LNER timetable in 1947 showed seven passenger trains per day to King's Lynn and six to Wisbech (seven on Saturdays) but none on a Sunday. Diesel multiple units were introduced on 3 November 1958, although some steam hauled passenger trains continued; but closure followed in September 1968, local freight having ceased on 19 April 1965.

The Wisbech and Upwell Tramway was one of those light railways to benefit from the 1896 Light Railways Act whose purpose was to make the construction of rural railways an easier task financially. Opened on 8 September 1884, the line was just over 5 miles long. Passenger services were withdrawn on 2 Januaruy 1928 but agricultural produce, the main reason for the line's existence, kept the railway in business until official closure on 20 May 1966.

The Lynn and Sutton Bridge Railway

This line was promoted in 1860 as the Mid-Eastern and Great Northern Junction Railway. Plans were announced for expansion via a spur at Lynn to the Dereham line and beyond. Financial problems restricted ambitions and an agreement was made which enabled the Great Northern Railway to operate the L&SB on completion in 1864. The line was subsequently operated by the Midland and Eastern Company which became part of the M&GN and formed a section of a major east-west trunk route. The line closed after the last trains on 28 February 1959 with the exception of the King's Lynn to South Lynn link.

Yaxham station looking north on 15 February 1955. The station was opened by the Norfolk Railway, with the line from Wymondham to Dereham to goods on 7 December 1846 and to passengers on 15 February 1847. The line was doubled in 1882 and facilities included a goods shed, cattle pen and sidings to the north of the crossing gates connecting to a granary. *(Stations UK)*

North Wootton station, looking towards Hunstanton, 1911. The main station building is on the right (Up) platform dating from the doubling of the line in 1898/9. The site is just over 3 miles from King's Lynn running across the flat coastal plain, some of it reclaimed land. In the absence of a goods shed or yard crane, freight facilities were always limited at this station. The Down line was lifted in the 1960s leaving single line working. *(HMRS/R. Hilton)*

Opposite, above: Dersingham station in 1911, looking north towards the main station building on the Up platform with the GER style canopy prominent. On the left, the timber signal box is a GER-type 7 design; whilst on the right beyond the cattle pens, is an end loading dock with the only available goods store nearby in the form of a small, lock-up goods shed. *(HMRS/R. Hilton)*

Opposite, below: Snettisham station looking north towards Hunstanton, 1911. The nearer of the two GER cattle vans is No 26080, built 1901. Above the other wagon in the distance (in the headshunt) is the gatekeeper's house. A substantial stone-built goods shed was available in Snettisham goods yard, the entrance to which is seen on the right where one of four sidings extended to Messrs Vynne and Everitt's granary. *(HMRS/R. Hilton)*

SONS

Hunstanton station looking towards the Sandringham Hotel, 1960s. The station layout is unusual in that the two island platforms diverged, hence the large spaces between buffer stops at the terminus end. *(Lens of Sutton)*

A general view of the station throat at Hunstanton looking towards King's Lynn, *c.* 1960. An unidentified Ivatt LMR 2–6–0 4MT stands adjacent to the turntable, a replacement in 1935 whose greater length enabled larger engines such as B17 class 4–6–0s to be turned and be available to work more heavily loaded excursion trains. The northlight roofed engine shed is behind the locomotive. The carriage sidings were lengthened in 1937 to accommodate the extra vehicles that increased holiday traffic bookings were encouraging. *(R. Carpenter)*

Docking station facing Heacham, 29 June 1936. This was the largest station on the West Norfolk Railway between Heacham and Wells and was just over 11 miles from Wells. An Up and Down platform were provided, the main building (in view) being on the Up side and built of local Carstone material. The local church contains memorials to the Hare family including Major Hare, one-time chairman of the West Norfolk Railway. (*H.C. Casserley*)

King's Lynn, 1911. The sidings shown wind round to the left to cross Estuary Road. To the right are the sheds belonging to Stanton's sawmill with some of their stock piled high to the left. *(HMRS/R. Hilton)*

A view across Alexandra Dock at King's Lynn, *c.* 1880. Coal wagons from the Peterborough area are prominent,

including those of R. Coller and Son and Messrs Beeby. The coal depot was operated by J.E. Cook. *(HMRS/R. Hilton)*

King's Lynn swing bridge leading from Alexandra Dock to Bentinck Dock, 1911. Bentinck Dock is to the left with J.T. Stanton and Co's timber yard featured again. *(HMRS/R. Hilton Collection)*

The reverse view of the previous picture looking south east across the combined road and rail bridge to Pilot Street and King's Lynn yard with many Midland Railway open wagons lined up. *(HMRS/R. Hilton Collection)*

Well coaled-up, No 5470, a Class J15 0–6–0 (nicknamed 'Black Goods'), stands stabled facing east outside King's Lynn running shed, 15 April 1947. The locomotive's rundown appearance and faintly visible NE insignia on the tender suggest a typical spell of extensive hard graft without much attention from the shed cleaning staff. *(H.C. Casserley)*

Ex-GNR Ivatt Class C12 No 67374, a design first introduced in 1898. No 67374 stands facing east on a middle road in King's Lynn station awaiting its next South Lynn shuttle service duty, 7 September 1957. The station was a replacement of an earlier terminus dating from Lynn and Ely Railway days and was a joint GER, MR and GNR venture. *(J. Edgington)*

South Lynn engine shed, 21 February 1959. Ivatt 4MT 2–6–0 No 43094 is on the right. The shed originally had two roads and held four engines. In 1895, two more roads were added. The shed was replaced late in the line's life in 1958 only to be closed in 1961. The 60 ft turntable did duty for those locomotives too long for turning at King's Lynn shed. *(Philip Kelley)*

The east-facing Down platform at Hillington boasting a well maintained summer garden display, July 1936. Opened on 16 August 1879, it was originally on a single line which was doubled in 1896 by the M&GN. Close to Sandringham Estate, the station enjoyed royal patronage and the waiting room was designated by the railway authorities as 'special'. *(H.C. Casserley)*

Travelling west, the LNER footplateman prepares to exchange the tablet permitting line occupation by the train beyond Massingham station, whose platform is visible beyond the signal box. The upper part of the box is a Midland Railway design but with a typical M&GN adaptation of a concrete block base. *(H.C. Casserley)*

Ex-M&GNR Class C 4–4–0 No 45 near Hillington on the 7.00 am Yarmouth to Peterborough on 4 July 1936, the year this loco was withdrawn. No 45 was supplied in 1894 from Sharp, Stewart and Co, since when rebuilding by the M&GN, particularly the provision of a stovepipe chimney, has affected the original pleasing design. *(H.C. Casserley)*

The ex-M&GN Type 1a signal box at South Lynn Junction, opened in April 1901 and closed on 11 November 1962. *(Philip Kelley)*

Class C 4–4–0 No 53 hurries the 2.38 pm South Lynn to Norwich train composed of a vintage collection of carriages near Thursford, 4 July 1936. No 53 was supplied to the M&GNR in 1896 from Sharp, Stewart and Co. This engine was the first of its class to be rebuilt with an altered boiler, cab and smokebox, radically changing its appearance. *(H.C. Casserley)*

Opposite, above: Ex-M&GNR Class C 4–4–0 near Thursford, 4 July 1936. Withdrawn in 1938, this locomotive retains its original MR-style cab but has been fitted with a short chimney. Apart from their smaller coupled wheels, this class followed closely the Midland Railway design of the late 1890s. *(H.C. Casserley)*

Opposite, below: A westbound goods train passes the tall somersault signal near Thursford, 4 July 1936. The locomotive, Class DA 0–6–0 No 86, is a Dubs and Co-built, Ivatt design intended primarily for the Great Northern Railway. The M&GNR have rebuilt their No 86 with a larger, extended boiler and a stovepipe chimney. *(H.C. Casserley)*

Sharp, Stewart & Co Class 4–4–0 No 54 of 1896 vintage stands in the July sunshine at South Lynn, 1936, the year prior to its withdrawal from traffic. The dark smokebox contrasts with the lighter tones of the rest of the

nachine which would have been painted umber at the time. The tender is a one-off special fitted specifically for vorking Yarmouth to Leicester and return. The tablet catcher is attached to the tender. *(H.C. Casserley)*

A shiny M&GN Sharp, Stewart & Co. Class C 4–4–0 No 4 stands at Melton Constable. The cab had been extended and a shorter chimney fitted by the time this loco was photographed in July 1936. The raised numeral on the rear splasher can be seen under this lighting. *(H.C. Casserley)*

M&GN Class D 0–6–0 No 61 simmers in the yard at Melton Constable on 28 May 1937, the year it became part of LNER stock. Constructed by Neilson & Co in 1896, it was built to the Johnson 2284 class Midland Railway design specifications and lasted in service until 1943. *(H.C. Casserley)*

M&GN Sharp, Stewart Class C 4–4–0 No 55 at Melton Constable taking water on 26 June 1929. Reboilered in 1925, this loco lasted in service until 1943 as LNER No 055. *(H.C. Casserley)*

M&GN Sharp, Stewart Class C 4–4–0 No 2 of 1894 stands at Melton Constable station, June 1929, prior to rebuilding with Belpaire boiler and removal of the Deeley parallel-style chimney seen here. M&GN ballast wagons appear in the background *(H.C. Casserley)*

0–6–0T No 099 at Melton Constable in May 1937 after it had been renumbered by the LNER and designated by them as Class J93. Officially a rebuilt class constructed at Melton Constable works, there was not much material used from the engines they replaced. *(H.C. Casserley)*

Sharp, Stewart & Co. M&GN Class C 4–4–0 stands by the water tower at Melton Constable shed at the front of a line of locomotives. To the right can be seen a rail-built buffer stop which dates back to a time in Eastern and Midland railway days, pre-1890. The photograph is dated 4 July 1936. *(H.C. Casserley)*

M&GN Class C 4–4–0 coaling at South Lynn running shed, adjacent to the east yard, 1 July 1936. This was one of the final batch of Class Cs delivered to the M&GN in 1899 from Beyer, Peacock & Co and this engine lasted until the year following this photograph. *(H.C. Casserley)*

Sharp, Stewart & Co Class C 4–4–0 No 46 approaches South Lynn Junction on the 1.45 pm from Yarmouth on 25 June 1929, whilst a tank engine shunts in the east yard to the right. The line to King's Lynn veers off to the right. *(H.C. Casserley)*

M&GN 0–6–0ST No 16A, the works pilot stands alongside the coal stack at Melton Constable, 26 June 1929. Built by Fox, Walker & Co (Bristol) in 1877 for the Yarmouth and Stalham Light Railway the engine originally carried the name *Stalham* and was without an enclosed cab. The livery appears to be plain black and it was not until 1936 that it was scrapped. *(H.C. Casserley)*

Opposite, below: The right hand tank engine at Melton Constable on 26 June 1929 is M&GN Class MR 0–6–0T No 16 which had the distinction of remaining in service throughout the LNER period and into BR days up until 1949. To the left is No 9, an ex-Lynn and Fakenham Railway 4–4–0T, then named *Fakenham*. The M&GN described the Class as 'B' and in 1909, 9 became 9A and was reserved for hauling Directors' and Engineers' inspection saloons until scrapped in 1932. *(H.C. Casserley)*.

Two passenger vehicles running on the ex-M&GN, April 1947, both photographed at South Lynn. The LMS and LNER transferred stock built at their respective carriage building works in 1935 prior to the LNER operational takeover. The top vehicle is an ex-LNWR gas-lit carriage dating from 1902 whilst the lower view shows an ex-MR corridor clerestory-roofed vehicle built at Derby in 1911. *(H.C. Casserley)*

Clenchwarton station looking west along the long straight stretch of permanent way towards Terrington, May 1938. Behind the photographer was the signalbox and to the left a typical M&GN waiting shelter. Behind the platform on the right was an end loading dock and two sidings to deal with the station's traffic in farm produce. Opened on 1 March 1866 as a single line station, it closed on 28 February 1959. *(H.C. Casserley)*

A Hudswell, Clark & Rogers-manufactured Class B 4–4–0T at Melton Constable on 26 June 1929. This was No 20A, originally a Yarmouth and North Norfolk Railway engine named *King's Lynn* and retained for working Directors' and Engineers' inspection saloons. 20A was withdrawn in 1931. *(H.C. Casserley)*

The Wisbech and Upwell Tramway was authorised in 1882 and built alongside the Wisbech to Outwell canal and public roads largely to transport fruit. Passengers were carried until 2 January 1928. In this view the 12.40

empty van train from Wisbech stands in Outwell yard behind LNER J70 0–6–0T Tram 7125, 25 June 1929. *(H.C. Casserley)*

By the date of this photograph, August 1958, the ex-LNER N7 class 0–6–2T had taken over the running of the South Lynn to King's Lynn push and pull trains. Here 69694 faces west with the road bridge in view behind the carriages. *(RAS Marketing)*

The crew of LNER Holden Class J17 0–6–0 5586 await their next move at Melton Constable station on 1 October 1946. *(F.A. Wycherley)*

Narborough looking towards King's Lynn, 1930s. This station was a crossing place on the King's Lynn to Dereham single line. The original East Anglian Railway building is on the left. Behind the photographer was a goods shed which in the 1950s was rented to Messrs R. Silcock and Sons for storing animal foodstuffs. The station closed to passengers on 7 September 1968. *(Barry Hoper Collection* per *B. Wilson)*

East Winch station looking towards King's Lynn, May 1968 – by which time the Down platform had been shortened. Poorly sited to serve any local village, the isolation of the location is readily seen in this view. The Up platform on the right, adjacent to the passing loop, was added in 1886 when resignalling became necessary. A Down refuge siding was positioned at the Swaffham end of the layout where there was also a goods yard. *(Gresley Society/L.R. Peters)*

7415
L N E R

L N E R

Ivatt 4MT 2–6–0 43148 is turned around ready for its next duty at Melton Constable, *c.* 1957. The Ransome and Rapier 70 ft vacuum operated design has replaced a turntable installed in 1884. The island platform in view separates the Great Yarmouth and Norwich lines. To the middle right is a staff messroom and a water standpipe dating back to the time of the Lynn and Fakenham Railway. *(R. Carpenter Collection)*

Opposite, above: LNER E4 Class 2–4–0 7415 leaves Wells-on-Sea, 26 June 1936. No 7415 was one of ten examples that were built at Stratford works in 1902 in a resumption of a building programme interrupted in 1896 when the class totalled ninety. The 2–4–0 wheel arrangement had become anachronistic by the 1930s and 7415 was withdrawn a year after being photographed although others survived well into BR days. *(H.C. Casserley)*

Opposite, below: LNER ex-Great Central Railway Class D9 4–4–0 6041 makes a spirited start away from Melton Constable on a Yarmouth to Leicester train, 13 March 1939. *(H.C. Casserley)*

The last surviving E4 2–4–0 62785 seen here at Burnham Market and displaying the lamp code above the buffers for an express train whilst it does duty on a Loco Club of Great Britain rail tour. This loco was destined to be preserved as part of the National Collection and restored to its original GER condition. At this stage, 12 July 1959, this was the only remaining part of the West Norfolk Railway where once block trains of cattle traffic had been marshalled for the trip to the London markets. *(B. Wilson/B. Hoper Collection)*

J69 0–6–0T 68566 waits at Stoke Ferry on the same LCGB tour (12 July 1959) as seen at Burnham Market (previous picture). Stoke Ferry lost its passenger service as early as 22 September 1930 but survived for goods until 19 April 1965. No 68566 spent many years allocated to South Lynn shed until the wholesale M&GN closure in 1959. Nicknamed 'Buckjumpers', the type was not uncommon on the Stoke Ferry branch, one of the class (7272) being responsible for hauling the last passenger train. *(B. Wilson/B. Hoper Collection)*

Class J17 0–6–0 65519 built in 1901 seen on 31 October 1959 passing Dereham Central Box, five months before it was withdrawn. It had been fitted with a replacement tender of greater water capacity from a withdrawn Class D16 4–4–0. Dereham Central Box of 1882 closed on 29 October 1969. *(B. Hoper Collection)*

Reggie Masters stands in the cab of Ivatt LNER Class J1 0–6–0 5006 at South Lynn, September 1948. The tablet catcher is prominent on the tender. *(Reginald Master's Collection, courtesy M&GN Circle)*

Porter Ernest Beckett poses for the photographer before cranking the handle of the 1-ton crane to assist in unloading a cultivator, East Rudham,1938. *(E. Beckett, courtesy M&GN Circle)*

Grimston Road station, 1930s, with Jack Marshall leaning on his bicycle alongside an ex-M&GN brake van and the view towards Fakenham beyond the level crossing. To the left is an original Lynn and Fakenham Railway water tank and in front of it the tablet apparatus. The station closed to passengers on 28 February 1959 and for goods in May 1968. *(M&GN Circle Collection)*

Many ex-M&GN stations prided themselves on their platform gardens and amongst the best in the 1920s and '30s was Gayton Road which won 'Best Kept Station' awards. Here Stationmaster Jack Bacon is dwarfed by the hollyhocks in the summer of 1928. *(G.R. Hayes, courtesy M&GN Circle)*

East Winch station with an Anglo-American Oil Co Ltd lorry standing on the level crossing opposite the signal box at the Dereham end of the station, 1920s. The rape seed oil for the station lamps was delivered in this fashion by the driver and his mate who stand either side of the station porter. *(Late Arthur Summers courtesy Alan Summers)*

An unidentified LNER Class J15 0–6–0 approaches Emneth station heading in the March direction with a trainload of vans, *c.* 1937. To the right the stationmaster's house is included in the main station building. GER remnants include the station bench and the station name board with typical late GER cutout letters and framing. The station has a long history, being in use by 1850, possibly earlier. Freight traffic ceased on 5 October 1964 followed by the end of passenger facilities on 9 September 1968. *(Stations UK)*

Abbey station on the Stoke Ferry branch looking towards Denver and the single-storey station building in 1911. In the goods siding some open wagons are sheeted over whilst a horse drawn cart stands alongside. The station was opened in August 1882, and its name was expanded to Abbey for West Dereham in 1886 but this did little to increase income. The establishment of a junction with the Wissington Light Railway (opened 1905) kept goods traffic alive until 1982, long after passenger trains ceased in 1930. *(HMRS/R. Hilton Collection)*

Downham looking towards Ely on a murky November day in 1911. On the left is a timber goods shed and malthouse. To the far right is a gas works and nearest the camera to the right is the Eagle Flour Mills with its private siding, a facility that the GER encouraged and supported both financially and with track laying in order to stimulate such local industries and thereby develop their own extra traffic. *(HMRS/R. Hilton)*

A wagon turntable at Downham Market, 1960s. A typical installation where maltings and other industrial sites sought access at right angles for wagon load traffic on to a main route. This example formerly had timber decking and the wooden post on the left acted as a buffer. To the right was Bennett and Son Ltd's maltings whilst other routes could be set for end loading bays. *(J.*

Manning, Wardle and Co. Ltd 0–6–0T 1532 *Newcastle*, built in 1901, stands at Wissington in 1964 on part of the 18-mile standard gauge light railway opened from Abbey and West Dereham in 1906. Originally the railway was built to develop the estate of A.J. Keeble and assist Fenland drainage plans. The opening of a sugar beet factory in 1924 assisted the income of the line until in 1957 the line closed north of Wissington. *(R.C. Riley)*

Melton Constable works, May 1937, six months after the LNER management had decided to take virtually all work away, causing great deprivation in what has been described as a railway village. The works were later used for War Department storage in 1939 and then for wagon sheet manufacture (1942), followed by a spell as a wagon and carriage repair works. *(H.C. Casserley)*

A westbound LNER tender locomotive at East Rudham, 16 April 1947. A footplateman watches the collection of the tablet which will make single line working safe for the train. *(H.C. Casserley)*

0–6–0T J70 Tram loco 68217 at Small Lode crossing approaches Upwell with the 12.45 pm from Wisbech, 25 August 1950. Footplatemen and schoolboy passenger pose for the camera, sixteen years before closure of the 7¾ mile route. *(H.C. Casserley)*

An ex-Eastern and Midland Railway horsebox with groom's compartment at the far end is being sorted by the shunter with his pole at the ready at Melton Constable, July 1936. *(H.C. Casserley)*

4

The Central Districts

Wymondham South Junction on 1 September 1968 looking west. Little has altered since the mid-1930s apart from a re-alignment of crossings on the Dereham branch to the right. The main line from Norwich continues onwards to Cambridge. The base of the station water tank is to the right along with the station garden. At one time to the right of the signalbox there was a coaling stage and turntable. *(R. Carpenter Collection)*

Ely to Norwich

The Ely to Norwich route crossed into Norfolk at Brandon and continued via Thetford to form the only main line across Central Norfolk. Brandon was the end-on junction between the Norfolk Railway, formerly the Norwich and Brandon Railway incorporated in 1844, and the Eastern Counties Railway. On 30 July 1845, the N&BR was opened on the same day as the Eastern Counties Railway's Newport to Brandon extension. London to Norwich services were operated immediately along a double tracked main line which had been diverted from its original route to make an intermediate station at Thetford.

Further importance was given to the line when the Trowse Bridge was completed, thereby allowing entry to Thorpe station and a junction with the Yarmouth and Norwich Railway.

The ECR leased the N&BR in May 1848 under a mutual agreement as Parliament would not allow a full amalgamation, leaving the N&BR nominally independent until the creation of the Great Eastern Railway in 1862. The introduction of management by the ECR coincided with an unhappy period for the line with a number of serious accidents occurring along its length, to such a degree that the Board of Trade investigators described the line as insecure and dangerous. Following this condemnation the infrastructure was given close attention at some expense and the situation improved.

Along the route, the towns of Thetford, Wymondham and Brandon all gained commercially through their connections to the railway. In addition to its function as a main line between London and Norwich, traffic from the Midlands and from various branch lines that were opened from the main line increased the importance of the N&BR route whilst Norwich (Thorpe) became the city's main terminus.

Under the LNER, during the Second World War, the line between Brandon and Norwich played an important strategic role serving air bases, training areas and storage depots alike. With the demise of steam traction and the decline in freight operations, the Ely to Norwich line has come to experience a revival in passenger train timings.

THETFORD TO SWAFFHAM BRANCH

In 1866, the Thetford and Watton Company was incorporated with authority to raise funds to construct a 9-mile line from Roudham Junction on the Ely to Norwich main line to Watton, opening to goods and passenger traffic in 1869. In the same year the line was planned to continue to Swaffham on the King's Lynn to Dereham line operated at the time by the GER, with whom the Watton and Swaffham Company were empowered to enter into agreement. Shortage of capital held up services until 1875, when financial help was obtained from the Thetford and Watton Company which eventually took over the working arrangements.

To reach Bury St Edmunds via a spur at Thetford Bridge proved too ambitious, and the GER baled out the lines by taking over the working in 1879, followed by a leasing arrangement in 1880 and then total absorption in 1898, the Thetford Bridge spur having been closed by the GER in 1880. Locally known as the 'Crab and Winkle' line the RAF base at Watton brought the line much traffic during the Second World War. The character of the line was expressed in the many prizes awarded to various stations on the branch for their exemplary platform garden displays. The whole route closed to passengers on 15 June 1964 with freight, particularly sugar beet, continuing between Watton and Swaffham only until 19 April 1965.

The River Waveney Line

The valley of the River Waveney offered the pioneer railway engineers an obvious route to link London with Norwich and Yarmouth and, as early as March 1845, two plans emerged and were brought before Parliament although neither was successful. Four months later, in July 1845, the Norfolk Railway's line from Trowse to Brandon via Thetford and Wymondham and the Eastern Counties line from Brandon to Ely, Cambridge and Newport were both opened, thereby offering a route from London through to Norwich and Yarmouth. The opening of these lines prompted Parliamentary wrangling between the Waveney Valley and Great Yarmouth Railway and the Norfolk Railway concerning proposals to build through the Waveney Valley, and all powers obtained with great effort by the Norfolk Railway through Parliament were allowed to lapse.

Eventually an Act of Incorporation in 1851 authorised a locally backed successor to the earlier scheme, entitled the Waveney Railway Company, to construct a 13-mile local line from Tivetshall station on the Eastern Union Railway to a terminus at Bungay. A further Act of 4 August 1853 authorised an extension to form a junction at Beccles with what was to become the East Suffolk Railway. Against a background of depressed money markets, progress was slow and the line had reached only as far as Harleston, which opened on 1 December 1855, worked by the Eastern Counties Railway which by this date had taken over the EUR. Worsening relations between the WVR and the ECR over management and financial matters, along with shortages of men and materials, brought a frustrating period, with delays in completing the contract to Bungay until 2 November 1860, intermediate stations having been opened at Homersfield and Earsham. An Act to

Wymondham South Junction on 1 September 1968, looking west. Little has altered since the mid-1930s apart from a re-alignment of crossings on the Dereham branch to the right. The main line from Norwich continues onwards to Cambridge. The base of the station water tank is to the right along with the station garden. At one time to the right of the signalbox there was a coaling stage and turntable. *(R. Carpenter Collection)*

authorise an increase in capital for the remainder of the route to Beccles was sought and finally obtained on 22 July 1861, by which time the GER had been formed and duly absorbed the line when it opened to Beccles on 2 March 1863.

Throughout its lifetime of operation, the Waveney Valley Railway provided a typical branch line service to the local community. In wartime, particularly the Second World War, its role was much extended through the siting of Air Ministry operations in its vicinity. However by the late 1940s, though reasonable in summer, ticket sales became uncommercial in the winter months and so the line closed to passenger services, at the time operated by Class F4 2–4–2Ts and J15 0–6–0s.

A Light Railway Order to enable the running of a freight service in a more economical fashion was introduced on 15 November 1954. This failed to achieve the necessary results, so that the route was closed between Harleston and Bungay in 1960, followed by the section from Bungay to Ditchingham in August 1964; then the remaining stump to Beccles closed on 19 April 1965, with the opposite end of the line following a year later, to complete the total closure on 18 April 1966.

WELLS-NEXT-THE-SEA BRANCH

In 1846 the Wymondham to Dereham section of this 33-mile branch was opened to goods and shortly after, in 1847, to passengers. The line was extended to Fakenham in 1849 and construction continued to Wells-on-Sea in 1857. The Norfolk Railway managed the southern section as far as Fakenham, beyond that a locally based company, the Wells and Fakenham Railway, were responsible.

Worked by the Eastern Counties Railway from inception until the GER was established and in control from 1862, the services remained very little changed until the 1960s, when the Wells to Dereham passenger service closed with effect from 5 October 1964 and many goods facilities were withdrawn along the whole of the branch. Through passenger traffic to King's Lynn via Dereham ceased on 7 September 1968, thereby rendering the Wymondham to Dereham section, already reduced to single line operation, vulnerable to closure. The passenger services of the remaining stretch were subsequently withdrawn on 4 October 1969.

Later, the southern part of the line saw re-opening attempts through sponsored excursions until the final freight services ran in April 1989.

GER No 1 Class 2–4–0 No 33, nicknamed the 'Little Sharpies', were predominantly used around the GER routes within Norfolk at the time of this photograph, 6 April 1910, particularly those radiating from Norwich. In this case the engine is standing at Wymondham Junction. *(LCGB/ K. Nunn Collection)*

The complex track layout at Swaffham in 1911 seen from the Junction signalbox just west of where the Thetford line via Holme Hale joined the Lynn and Dereham. The view is looking towards King's Lynn and the station buildings. On the left, the two road wooden engine shed is unusually at right angles to the adjoining main line and is served by a 45° turntable. In the background is a granary and behind the water tower on the left is an oil tank belonging to the Anglo-American Oil Company. *(HMRS/R. Hilton)*

Ditchingham station and signal box, *c.* 1910. Ditchingham was situated on the final section of the single line Waveney Valley Railway opened on 1 March 1863. To the right the line proceeded to Beccles via Ellingham and Geldeston. The station building was substantial, as was a goods shed, out of picture to the left. Closed to passengers on 5 January 1953, it was kept open for sand and gravel traffic until April 1964. *(B. Hoper Collection)*

Geldeston station looking towards Beccles, 12 October 1911. The station building is obscured by the substantial brick goods shed. As an emergency economy measure in the First World War, Geldeston was closed to all traffic on 22 May 1916 then re-opened and downgraded to a halt in that autumn. It regained its status as a full station in 1922. *(HMRS/R. Hilton Collection)*

Pulham Market opened on 1 December 1855 as Pulham St Magdalene with a train service from Tivetshall to Harleston worked by the Eastern Counties Railway. It was renamed Market in March 1856. The goods train is heading towards Pulham Mary and will pass a siding laid in 1915 to serve an airship station. In spite of the LNER on the poster board, the date is 31 May 1952. *(D.E. Shepherd* per *B. Wilson)*

The disused station at Redenhall looking towards Harleston in 1951. It opened in January 1861 following the November 1860 extension of the Waveney Valley route from Harleston to Bungay. However, after only five years service, Redenhall was closed. *(B.D.J. Walsh)*

PULHAM ST MARY

LNER Class E4 2–4–0 No 7492 at Dereham on 29 June 1936, looking south towards the central signal box on the left beyond the ex-GER bracket signal. No 7492 became BR No 62787 and was withdrawn in July 1956. *(H.C. Casserley)*

Opposite, above: Ellingham station at closure, January 1953. A small, one platform station with one siding, it had a grounded brake coach body serving as a goods shed-cum-store. *(B.D.J. Walsh)*

Opposite, below: Pulham St Mary station looking east in 1951. It was named Pulham Mary from 1866 until it reverted to its previous name in June 1894. Passenger service ceased from 5 January 1953 but goods continued until April 1966. The architectural design incorporated in this and other station buildings on the Waveney Valley route is worthy of note. *(B.D.J. Walsh)*

Two views of Fakenham station looking towards Wells-on-Sea, 1 September 1955. Ex-LNER Class D16/3 4–4–0 No 62577 arrives with the 12.53 pm Wells to Norwich train. Opened on 20 March 1849, Fakenham became 'East' to distinguish it from the ex-M&GN station in the town in September 1948. Passenger trains stopped running on 3 October 1964 and the line northwards was completely closed on 6 November of the same year. The Eastern Counties Farmers Ltd grain warehouse is in view, built upon land once occupied by a cattle dock. Gas lighting on the platform is still evident and the canopied roof is above a construction dating from 1859, as is the slate-roofed porters' and lamp room. *(R.M. Casserley)*

Ex-LNER Class E4 2–4–0 No 62793 of Norwich shed waits in the area of the turntable and engine shed at Dereham probably to take away a load of ash and clinker, August 1953. No 62793 has the extended cab with side window protection fitted to those engines of the class transferred to the North Eastern section of the LNER in 1935. This gave the footplatemen better conditions in a colder environment. *(L.R. Peters/courtesy Gresley Society)*

Ex-LNER Class J15 0–6–0 No 65472 stands outside Dereham shed on 19 September 1953. In BR days Dereham was a sub-shed to Norwich and the normal total allocation was eight or nine locos, the largest being D16/3 4–4–0s with a J15 and three J17 0–6–0s for freight work. The steam shed closed on 19 September 1955 but, prior to being demolished, was used for stabling lightweight Derby-built diesel railcars when they took over the local passenger services. *(F.A. Wycherley)*

Cawston station looking south west in 1962. This route from Wroxham to County School was opened as part of the East Norfolk Railway's barrier to competition from any independent development of a railway from Norwich to Aylsham. The line opened to Cawston on 1 September 1880. Passenger trains ceased on 15 September 1952 but freight facilities lasted until 31 October 1966. Through traffic lasted even longer when a connection was formed to the ex-M&GNR line at Themelthorpe, thereby routing traffic through Cawston until the early 1980s. *(Stations UK)*

The stylish architecture adopted for stations on the first and third built sections of the Waveney Valley Railway is shown in this view of Harleston on 30 September 1956 on the occasion of the Railway Enthusiasts' Club visit. Harleston opened on 1 December 1855 and closed to passengers on 5 January 1953, followed by total closure of the Bungay to Harleston section on 1 February 1960 – whilst the route to Tivetshall lasted until April 1966. *(R.M. Casserley)*

Ex-LNER Class J15 0–6–0 No 65447 heads the Railway Enthusiasts' Club special at Harleston station looking east, 30 September 1956. A Light Railway Order had been implemented on November 1954 as a final but failed attempt to keep the line economically viable. *(RAS/Photomatic)*

Homersfield station after closure, 29 June 1969. This was one of the intermediate stations on the Harleston to Bungay section of the Waveney Valley line opened on 2 November 1860. Flooding of the River Waveney washed away most of the platform and damaged the track at Homersfield in August 1912. The single platform without goods facilities allowed the station to be run as a halt in its final days until closure in 1960. *(J. Edgington)*

Brandon goods yard with the station beyond to the west, October 1911. Cattle pens show up on the left and behind is the chimney of a small sawmill. The water tower to the left of the goods sheds is a reminder of Brandon's days as the main railway works of the Norwich and Brandon Railway. When the latter became part of the Norfolk Railway, Brandon formed an end-on junction between the NR and the ECR. Brandon closed to goods on 18 April 1966 and became an unmanned halt on 7 March 1967. *(HMRS/R. Hilton)*

Brandon station looking east, *c.* 1924, as a Scout troop prepare to board their train hauled by ex-GER Class T19R (LNER D13) No 7700 with the splashers covering the 7 ft driving wheels quite prominent. A footbridge connected the staggered platforms. *(Stations UK)*

Wymondham station and yard, 1911, looking west with the signals for the Dereham branch just visible above the footbridge beyond the main station building. The line of privately owned wagons stands on a siding leading to the coal drops of J. Coller and Sons. The goods shed on the right was originally entered from a wagon turntable at right angles but in *c.* 1876 a side arch in the shed was unbricked to allow more convenient access. *(HMRS/R. Hilton Collection)*

GER 2–4–0 numbered No 1 and also classified No 1. The Sharp, Stewart and Co-built locomotive is seen here at Wymondham on 15 April 1911, taking on water. The advertisement alongside the fence is a reminder of a local industry. *(LCGB/K. Nunn)*

Thetford station, 9 May 1953. Ex-LNER Class J15 0–6–0 No 65472 on a typical duty heads the 1.45 pm train to Swaffham. Behind the loco is an elderly ex-main line carriage, also a typical feature of Norfolk's branch lines in the 1950s. In this instance the vehicle is ex-GCR, nicknamed a 'Barnum' (after Barnum and Bailey's travelling circus, popular at the time (1912) of manufacture of the open brake carriage). *(H.C. Casserley)*

Opposite, above: GER 2–4–0 loco No 1 of Class No 1 on the 1.58 pm Wells to Forncett train passes a level crossing near Wymondham, 15 April 1911. *(LCGB/K. Nunn)*

Opposite, below: Thetford West signal box looking east, showing the junction between the Norwich via Wymondham line to the left and the Bury St Edmunds route to the right, 17 November 1911. Thetford was opened by the Norwich and Brandon railway on 29 July 1845. *(HMRS/R. Hilton Collection)*

The London end of Thetford station taken from the cattle dock, 17 October 1911. The station signal box is to the left whilst, on the right, the wooden shed contained coal drops to facilitate loading in the yard below. The crane behind the loading gauge has a conical iron roof to keep the operator out of the rain. *(HMRS/R. Hilton Collection)*

Thetford station from the northern end, 31 March 1962. The RCTS ran a commemorative tour to celebrate 100 years of the GER. In the distance BR Britannia Pacific No 70003 *John Bunyan* has taken over the train from Ex-LNER Class J17 No 65567 (now preserved and the last steam loco at Norwich shed). No 65567 took over the train from the Britannia at Norwich (Victoria) and journeyed via Thorpe, Dereham and Swaffham to Thetford. *(B.P. Hoper Collection)*

A three coach Swaffham train at Thetford, *c.* 1955, being double headed by ex-LNER Class E4 2–4–0 No 62789 and Class D16/3 No 62601. The extra motive power is likely to be as a result of an unbalanced loco roster and to avoid a light engine movement. *(R. Carpenter Collection)*

Thetford station, 18 April 1949. Ex-LNER Class F6 2–4–2T still with the number allocated to it by the LNER, 7246, has arrived from Bury St Edmunds on the 4.23 pm passenger service. *(J. Edgington)*

Kimberley Park signal box, 4 December 1965. The branch had been singled on 13 June 1965 and the box became superfluous, trainmen being left to operate the level crossing gates. In the background demolition of the goods yard has started, but the line remained open for goods some twenty years after it had closed to passengers. *(N.D. Mundy/Courtesy RCTS)*

Tivetshall Junction station looking south, 31 May 1952. Ex-LNER Class F4 2–4–2T No 67167 stands next to the water crane in the Waveney Valley branch platform. By this date the Worsdell Class F4s were dwindling in number and 67167 went to the scrapyard shortly after this photograph was taken. *(D.E. Shepherd, courtesy B.P. Hoper)*

Tivetshall Junction looking north, 8 October 1960. Worsdell ex-GER 0–6–0, classified by the LNER as Class J15, No 65469 stands in the Waveney Branch platform having been well turned out by its home shed at Norwich to work the special train. *(B. Wilson, courtesy B.P. Hoper)*

The station nameboard on the Down platform with part of the goods shed visible behind. The station opened with the extension of the Ipswich to Norwich line to Norwich Victoria in 1849 and achieved added importance when the Waveney Valley route opened in sections to Beccles between 1855 and 1863. Closure (passengers) took place on 18 April 1966 followed by goods in November of that year. *(D.E. Shepherd, courtesy B.P. Hoper)*

Wretham and Hockham station looking towards Thetford, 31 August 1955. The use of flint in the stationmaster's house with booking office alongside is similar to other stations on the Thetford and Watton Railway route. A signal box controlled the level crossing at the end of the single platform. *(R.M. Casserley)*

Opposite, above: Holme Hale station looking south, *c.* 1937. The station building was of similar brick and flint construction to other intermediate stations on the Thetford to Swaffham branch but a mirror image design to that at Wretham and Hockham. The signal box was only brought into use to control the movements concerning the goods yard, in view beyond the ex-GER signal. *(Stations UK)*

Opposite, below: A second view of Holme Hale station in August 1955 taken from the carriage of a train bound for Swaffham before the passenger service ceased with the 9.21 pm from Thetford on Saturday 15 June 1963. *(R.M. Casserley)*

HOLME HALE
HOLME HALE

Ex-LNER Class D16/3 4–4–0 62544 at Norwich shed (32A) on February 22 1959. Built in March 1903 for the GER as a Class S46 it became Class D15 on the LNER. This locomotive was withdrawn in November 1959. Behind is a Gresley Class K3 2–6–0. *(Philip Kelley)*

Ex-LNER Class D16/3 No 62610 of Norwich shed has the right of way signalled by the ex-GER signal gantry as it hauls the 12.10 pm Norwich to King's Lynn, 12 May 1953. The carriage next to the locomotive is a Gresley designed full brake intended for parcels traffic on the LNER. *(Philip Kelley)*

Ex-LNER Class D16/3 4–4–0 62606 at King's Lynn shed (31C) on 21 February 1959. These engines were nicknamed 'Clauds' after Lord Claud Hamilton, chairman of the GER when the class was first introduced. By 1959, the 'Clauds' were seeing out the steam era on many secondary Norfolk lines, but in the past they had become famous for their haulage of the top GER train, the 'Norfolk Coast Express', whose timings between Liverpool Street and Cromer were not bettered until the introduction of the Britannia class in 1951. No 62606 retains the decorative splashers over the driving wheels and the unusual feature of a carriage-type drop window in the cab. *(Philip Kelley)*

Ashwellthorpe station looking north west. The station was situated on a cut-off route between Forncett and Wymondham built to ease traffic congestion at Norwich. In this view, *c.* 1939, the platforms are still gas lit and the nameboard is a late GER pattern. Opened in May 1881, the architectural style of the two-storey

stationmaster's house has echoes in its brickwork patterns of the earlier 1860s style of GER building. Passenger services ceased from 10 September 1939 but freight continued until 4 August 1951. *(Stations UK)*

In a dingy state, ex-LNER Class J15 0–6–0 No 65417 stands on the turntable at Norwich, its home shed, 2 September 1951. A B1 4–6–0 No 61041 is alongside the coaling tower. *(Philip Kelley)*

Ex-LNER Class B17/2 4–6–0 No 61610 *Honingham Hall* at Norwich shed on 22 February 1959. No 61610 was a Stratford shedded locomotive for much of the 1950s but when photographed it was based at Yarmouth Beach shed, later to be withdrawn from Cambridge in January 1960. *(Philip Kelley)*

BR notices at Norwich City station (February 1959) detailing the withdrawal of train services on the ex-M&GN lines. BR had concluded that only one route across Norfolk was necessary and the ex-GER route from the west via March, Manea and Thetford to Norwich was chosen. *(Philip Kelley)*

Hunslet-built Diesel Mechanical 0–6–0 No 11161 at Norwich shed when newly introduced on 21 April 1957. *(Philip Kelley)*

A view from the terminal end of Norwich Thorpe station on 1 October 1955. Britannia Class 7MT Pacific No 70042 *Lord Roberts* has arrived on the 10.30 am from Liverpool Street whilst D16/3 No 62555 stands at the head of a local train. *(Philip Kelley)*

Britannia class 7MT 4–6–2 No 70035 *Rudyard Kipling* eases the Down 'Broadsman' into Norwich Thorpe, 19 July 1954. The service was introduced in 1950 and by 1952 was offering a 145-minute Down journey. *(Philip Kelley)*

Ex-LNER B12/3 No 61568 awaits the 'right away' from the guard on the 2.52 pm Norwich to Cromer at Norwich Thorpe, 12 May 1953, with BR standard Mark 1 carriages in evidence behind the locomotive. On the engine's buffer beam can just be seen the unique Eastern Region custom of identifying the locomotive's class details. *(Philip Kelley)*

Class L1 2–6–4T No 67788 is seen from the vantage point of the Carrow Road bridge as it heads a train from Cromer towards Norwich Thorpe station off the Wensum Junction line. The Edward Thompson designed locomotive was relatively modern when the photograph was taken on 2 September 1951, the class being originally introduced in 1947. *(Philip Kelley)*

Norwich Thorpe, 2 September 1951. An engineman looks back along his train from the cab of ex-LNER Class K1 2–6–0 No 62018 of Cambridge (31B) shed. The service is the 2.34 pm to Liverpool Street via Cambridge. *(Philip Kelley)*

Norwich City engine shed and signalbox, 1950s. *(Philip Kelley)*

Ex-GER 0–6–0 No 564, later LNER J15 No 7564, then BR No 65462 on its first steaming since restoration in preservation on the North Norfolk Railway at Sheringham, 21 May 1977. A preserved diesel railbus stands in the background. *(Philip Kelley)*

M&GN somersault signals on a concrete post guard the exit from Norwich City station, 21 April 1954. The depot was a sub-shed of Melton Constable (32G) and was occupied at the time by ex-LNER D16/3 locos Nos 62617 and 62578 and J69 0–6–0T No 68625. *(Philip Kelley)*

Left: An ex-M&GN concrete post somersault signal at South Lynn contrasts with an LNER standard upper quadrant at South Lynn, 21 February 1959. *(Philip Kelley)*

Fakenham West, 21 February 1959, looking east from the station footbridge. *(Philip Kelley)*

Fakenham West crossing at the very end of the ex-M&GN'S operations on 21 February 1959, looking towards Yarmouth Beach. BR appended the West to Fakenham (M&GN) to distinguish it from the ex-LNER station which became East, both name changes occurring in September 1949. An Ex-M&GN Up home signal protected the crossing and the approach to the station. *(Philip Kelley)*

Ex-GER, ex-LNER Class J69/1 0–6–0T No 68499 stands outside King's Lynn shed on 21 February 1959 just prior to its closure. *(Philip Kelley)*

Ivatt Class 4MT No 43089, 31 October 1959, propelling the 1.35 pm 'Saturdays only' to King's Lynn into the Up platform at Swaffham from the siding nicknamed 'The Hole', where the train had been shunted on arrival from King's Lynn in the morning. By this date these two services were the only remaining steam hauled passenger trains between King's Lynn and Dereham. *(B. Wilson, courtesy B.P. Hoper)*

GER Trespassers sign. *(Philip Kelley)*

The Down working of the 'Broadsman' from London, minus headboard, reaches Wroxham station, 12 May 1953, with ex-LNER B1 61044 of Norwich shed in charge. From 1959 this train became the only weekday through working to Liverpool Street station, before ceasing altogether during the week in 1962. *(Philip Kelley)*

Acknowledgements

Thanks are owed to:
The late C.S. Bayes, Bryan Blaxall, Lyn D. Brooks, Roger Carpenter, Richard Casserley, Andrew Clayton, Nigel Digby, Great Eastern Railway Society, Paul Goldsmith, Graham Kenworthy, Historical Model Railway Society, R. Joby, R. Lock, Lens of Sutton, Frank D. Simpson, Graham Stacey (RAS Marketing), Alan Summers, B.D.J. Walsh, Bryan Wilson.

A number of enthusiasts have assisted me greatly with contributions to the photographic content, adding to information contained in the captions, and have compiled and made available an archive that may be accessed by members of the Midland and Great Northern Railway Circle and The Great Eastern Railway Society. Any errors and omissions are otherwise entirely my own.

Bibliography

Books

Branch Line Index, compiled by G.C. Lewthwaite (Branch Line Society, 1991)
British Railways Atlas and Gazetteer (Ian Allan Publishing, 1973)
A Guide to the M&GN Jt Railway, Nigel J.L. Digby (Ian Allan Publishing)
Oxford Companion to British Railway History, Simmons and Biddle (Oxford University Press,1997)
Locomotives of the LNER (RCTS, 1970)
Locomotives of the M&GN, Alan M. Wells. (HMRS)
The Lynn and Dereham Railway, S.C.Jenkins MA, (The Oakwood Press)
A Regional History of the Railways of Great Britain, Vol 5 D.I. Gordon (David and Charles, 1977)
The Wells-Next-The-Sea Branch, S.C. Jenkins MA, (The Oakwood Press)

Periodicals

Backtrack (Atlantic Transport Publishers)
British Railway Journal (Wild Swan Publications)
British Railway Journal, Special Great Eastern Edition (Wild Swan Publications)
British Railways Illustrated (Irwell Press)
Bylines (Irwell Press)
GERS Journal and Information packs (Great Eastern Railway Society)
HMRS Journal (Historical Model Railway Society)
Locomotives Illustrated (Ian Allan Publishing)
Midland and Great Northern Bulletin, (M&GN Circle)
Railway Magazine (Ian Allan Publishing)
Railway Observer (RCTS)
Railways South East (Railways SE)
Steam Days (Redgauntlet Publications)
Trains Illustrated (Ian Allan Publishing)